SAVE MY CHILDREN

AN ASTONISHING TALE OF SURVIVAL AND ITS
UNLIKELY HERO

LEON KLEINER

EDWIN STEPP

ISBN 9789493056527 (ebook)

ISBN 9789493056510 (paperback)

ISBN 9789493056572 (hardback)

Publisher: Amsterdam Publishers, The Netherlands

info@amsterdampublishers.com

Save My Children is part of the series Holocaust Survivor Memoirs World War II

Winner of the International Impact Book Awards 2022 in the category Life Experiences

Cover photo: The Kleiner family before the war. From left to right: Edek, Pearl "Pepi," Tusia, Izak "Zunio," and Leon Kleiner

CONTENTS

This book is dedicated to my two daughters Susan and Nina, my grandchildren Jamie, Danielle, Carly, Drew and Xander, and to my great grandson Liev Max.

In memory of David

Our son, and a loving brother and uncle

INTRODUCTION

This story is a remarkable tale of survival against all odds. It's a suspenseful tale of flight from unimaginable terror; filled with unlikely twists of fate that enabled the hunted to escape their murderous hunters. It's a chronicle of the amazing transformation and redemption of a man once filled with hate and violence and how he made the ultimate sacrifice to save people he once sought to kill.

But this isn't fiction or fantasy. It happened. So, most importantly, this story is a dire warning that hatred, bigotry and racism can lead to destruction, violence and genocide. It is a sad fact that human history is replete with examples of ethnic, religious and national 'cleansing.' But even so, many never learn from it and, unfortunately, these evils always come back to haunt us again.

Even though numerous personal stories of the Holocaust have been told, there remain those today who would deny that it happened or, even worse, not see the evil in it. We cannot allow the reality—and the lesson of that reality—to be forgotten. We must teach every succeeding generation that human nature can be exploited by evil men to unleash the most horrible crimes against innocent people.

With so much written and documented about this black period of human history—why is another book necessary? Why do I feel I have to tell my story? Isn't it just like so many others?

Miep Gies, the Dutch woman who was instrumental in bringing to light one of the first personal stories the world heard of these dark times—that of Anne Frank and her family—later wrote: "Anne cannot, and should not, stand for the many individuals whom the Nazis robbed of their lives. Each victim had his or her own ideals and outlook on life; each victim occupied a unique, personal place in the world and in the hearts of his or her relatives and friends. In their racial madness, Hitler and his accomplices tried to claim just the opposite: they portrayed the Jews [and many other groups] as a faceless enemy even as they annihilated six million individuals, extinguished six million individual lives."

Gies was right. Each individual story is crucially important to give faces, dimension, and reality to the numbers that are otherwise faceless, flat and incomprehensible. And the events recorded here are not just my story. It is just as much the story of one who ultimately gave his life to save us. A man without whom we couldn't have survived and eventually prospered. It is also an essential piece of the entire horrible puzzle of the Holocaust. His story—our story—offers a glimmer of hope that it is possible for people to change and emerge even from deep-seated and entrenched prejudices and hatred.

I haven't spoken a lot about my experiences during the Holocaust, but I have been asked to give a few speeches. When I've accepted the invitations, the speeches were short, and I mainly spoke about my friends, my childhood friends. I remember their names and what they looked like and I preferred to talk about them rather than speak about myself. There was Jancio Landau—a skinny, rather tall kid; Zenek Meiberger—a chubby boy who loved to read books; Zyga Francus—he was the class bully; Sala Schwartz—she looked like a doll to me, porcelain skin and so frail; Nunio Krasucki— a very good looking boy, except for acne on his face; Fela Miler—I had a crush on her. She was my first encounter with 'puppy love.'

And then there was Rysiek Lewinkron. His was a very sad story indeed. He was an only child whose parents refused to endure the hunger, the daily threat of death and the indignities of ghetto life. Rysiek and his parents committed suicide in the ghetto of Tarnopol.

Rysiek was not the only one of my friends from Tarnopol to perish. At the end of the war I discovered that none of my schoolmates, my playmates and my other friends from there managed to survive, neither them nor their families.

My sadness that so many of them didn't survive has always gripped me. They were only children, innocent and filled with so much potential. And there is the guilt that comes naturally with my survival. So, their remembrance for me is vital.

I've thought about documenting my story many times. But somehow it never came to fruition. In fact, when Stephen Spielberg started his Shoah Foundation interviews, I was contacted by the organizers and was asked to do an interview. At the time, I happened to be visiting Los Angeles where the foundation is based. When they called me, we made a date to do it at my daughter's house where I was staying.

The day we arranged for the interview was a Saturday morning. But when that morning finally came, I awoke, and a sense of fear gripped me. I got up and I said, "I can't do it." I wasn't ready to relive the terrible events even though they were over 50 years ago. I just wasn't capable; I couldn't bring myself to go through with it. For whatever reason, I got up that morning and I said, "I don't want to do it. I just can't."

So, I called and canceled the interview, apologizing for my lack of fortitude to recount the story. From that day forward, I felt as if I had failed a duty to add to the surmounting evidence against one of the greatest evils in all of human history. I have carried that weight for almost 20 years, and something in the back of my mind has taunted me, urging me to try again.

My story is also the story of the survival of my family. At the climax of this narrative, I was in very close quarters with my aunt, my brother and my sister and her boyfriend, the only ones of our immediate family to be delivered safely at the end of the war.

Both my brother and my sister took their turn to record their stories with the Shoah Foundation. Their stories, of course, were very similar to mine, and I was so glad they had the courage to sit for the many hours required to get them recorded. But I have some things to add to their record. During our ordeal, they were both older than me. My brother and sister were in their mid-teens preparing to enter adulthood. I was a young boy who couldn't fully understand how the world could go so mad so quickly. The war robbed me of a happy childhood, but I was one of the fortunate ones. Others were robbed of their lives and never had the opportunity that I had to prosper in spite of the terrible events. I came to believe that it was important for the nuances of my story to be told. It's a different perspective from theirs. It's one of a young boy coming of age in a world being destroyed rather than one open to limitless possibilities. The tragic murders of the young and innocent of that war may be the greatest crime. So many of my young friends were murdered and never had a chance to tell their stories.

In early 2017 I lost my brother. My sister died in 2010. While we struggled through our terrible ordeal, we couldn't have imagined the full and prosperous lives we would lead after the war. As I write this book, I have just turned 90. My brother lived to be 94 and my sister 87 years old. Yet their passing was very sad for me and I felt a great loss when they died. I know my years are also growing short and my story and those of the young innocents and this remarkable man who transformed from a rabid antisemite to our protector needs telling.

Although my brother and sister recorded their memories of it in their video interviews with the Shoah Foundation, our story has never been written down or published. So, I have decided that it would be important for me to contribute to the historical record in that way.

Here then are my memories of this extraordinary story of survival.

1 MY BIRTHPLACE - A HISTORY OF HATRED

None of us is given the choice of our time or place of birth. Even if we were, what assurance of making the right decision would there be? Had this power been granted to me, I am quite certain I would have taken my chances with vastly different options than what fortune delivered. But that sentiment comes only by looking back at my long life and the few years in the place that defined it most: 1939–1945 in eastern Poland.

As a young boy, I couldn't have been happier with the hand that fate had dealt me. But as the world descended into the darkness of World War II, I couldn't have been more vexed by it. There was no more unfortunate lot than being a Jew in Eastern Europe in that decade. For those long years I was put in situations over and over again with seemingly no odds for escape. Yet through all the horror, I found myself at the right time and place to elude death. Millions of my fellow Jews had no such luck. So as much as I wonder what my life would have been like if I had been born in a different place and time, I realize that I defied all the odds—and ultimately, I was most fortunate.

The time was August of 1928 and the place was a small city called Tarnopol. Then it was part of Poland, but today it is one of the major cities located within the boundaries of western Ukraine. If you research it now you will most likely find the Ukrainian spelling for it, Ternopol. But we will refer to it by its Polish name throughout the book, as we will for most of the other places that were a part of my story.

At the time of my birth, Tarnopol was a city of about 50,000 people and almost half of them were Jews. The city today has a population of about a quarter of a million people. Almost none of them are Jews. For hundreds of years before it became known as Tarnopol, there had been settlements along the Seret River. It was given its name in 1540 when Jan Amor Tarnowski, a high-ranking commander of the Polish army, was granted the right to establish a fortification as a line of defense against the Tatars. The name 'Tarnopol' derives from the combination of his last name with the Greek word for city, 'polis.' But the Ukrainians who eventually took control of it say that the name in Ukrainian means "a field covered with thorns."

As a child I had a much different picture of the city. It was nothing like a field of thorns; on the contrary, I considered it to be quite a pleasant place. It was buzzing with excitement. The streets were lined with bustling shops and restaurants, and the people showed a great love for music, art and lively culture. My vision of my birthplace had nothing in common with the hostile image painted by the Ukrainian etymology. But little did I know what lay ahead. For me, and for the people that I loved most, Tarnopol would soon become a nightmare beyond proportion—one that would make a field of thorns look like a bed of roses.

The history of Jews interspersed among the peoples of Europe had been a long one of uneasy acceptance and tolerance punctuated often by hatred and violence. The earliest records of Jews arriving in the area of Tarnopol and in Galicia, the broader region of eastern

Poland and western Ukraine to which the city belongs, date from the 14th century. Over the course of the next two hundred years, Jews began to settle in these areas in several successive waves. While they were sometimes encouraged to settle in the region under the protection of ruling powers in the region, some instances of Jewish migration were spurred by persecution and forced exile. The Spanish Inquisition, for example, was one significant cause of Jewish flight into Eastern Europe. Jews fleeing Spain and Portugal found their way to Tarnopol. Later, other forced exiles contributed to rapid population growth in the area. In the early 16th century, the Jewish population in eastern Poland was only about a half percent of the total population. However, by the beginning of the 17th century, it is estimated that over 500,000 Jews had arrived, making up about five percent of all inhabitants. There is little doubt that when Tarnopol was founded in 1540, Jews were some of the first people to make their homes there.

Since the city sat at a confluence of several competing ethnicities and nationalities, it seemed to always be caught in ongoing border wars. The Poles, Russians, Swedes, Austrians, Hungarians, Tatars and Turks would all lay claim to the territory around Tarnopol and fought each other for it many times. As a result, the economy waxed and waned over the next four hundred years. antisemitism would also rise and fall with each wave of war and the resulting financial hardships. But it was always present, even in peaceful times, seething under the surface and ready to explode when the Gentile people there needed a scapegoat for their problems.

But in the Tarnopol that I knew as a boy, one with as many Jews as Gentiles, times were good. Its brutal history was a long-forgotten thing of the past. My father's business savvy and hard work had created a prosperous life for my family and me. We were upper middle class and I look back on those times and realize we were spoiled. We encountered antisemitism occasionally but for the most part we lived peacefully alongside non-Jews. Many of them frequented my father's store and were pleasant and kind. In those circumstances, the belief that humanity had advanced out of the dark ages of tribalism and entered into to a Renaissance of civility was easy to come by.

Perhaps we were blindsided by the promises that came with an increasingly modernized world. With the rapid technological and scientific achievements, was it too easy to believe that we were following a linear path of progress and advancement in social values too? World War I was called the "war to end all wars" and after the devastation that it brought, there was great hope that the world could find a way to overcome differences in peaceful ways.

To some degree, my father fell victim to this thinking, as I will reveal later. It prevented him from acting to get us out of the way of the coming storm, even though plentiful signs were there. Unfortunately, we learned all too soon that technological progress did nothing to solve the failings of human nature. The past foreshadowed a different story, one stained with blood and ravaged by destruction, a story that has repeated its unfortunate plot line far too many times. Yet even in the face of this long history of murder and oppression, no one could have foreseen the scope and scale of the hideous events to come.

2 A WONDERFUL CHILDHOOD

I was the youngest of three children. The oldest—my brother Edek —was five years older, and my sister Tusia was four years older than me. My father's name was Izak, but his family and closest friends knew him as 'Zunio,' an affectionate nickname that developed through a playful distortion of his real name. My mother's name was Pearl, but she was also known best by an affectionate nickname. Her family and closest friends called her 'Pepi.'

My father was originally from a town called Stanisławów, situated just a little south of Tarnopol. It was a provincial place and he grew up in very modest circumstances. To make a living, his father bought and sold all kinds of products in the local market. When my father reached adulthood, he was conscripted into the Austrian army and sent off to Vienna. He wasn't happy about serving in the military, but he enjoyed life in Vienna. One of Europe's largest cities at the time, it was an exciting place and no doubt gave my father an expanded view of the world that helped him become successful. Living there also gave him a great appreciation for art, culture and the finer things in life. He was committed to making sure my siblings and I developed the same love and provided us with many opportunities to do so. We were all given music lessons and were encouraged to perform.

But the most important event for him in Austria was meeting my mother. I am sure they were drawn to each other by the fact that they had grown up so close to one another. My mother was from a small town called Tluste. It was about 100 kilometers directly east of Stanisławów. Her father owned a bakery there and was a pious Jew. He was one of the most respected men in the area and, as a result, his business thrived.

It was a safe and beautiful place to grow up and I am sure my mother always felt strong ties to her home. But as a young woman, my mother had always longed to get out and see the world. Tluste was so small—not quite small enough to be called a village, but not quite big enough to be a town. So, when she was old enough, she pleaded with her father to let her travel and see what life was like in a major city. I don't know why she chose Vienna but it isn't difficult to speculate. Other big cities were closer, Kiev, Warsaw and even Budapest. As large as those cities were, the Viennese culture was considered at the time to be at the pinnacle of human achievement in every realm. There was no city in the world that could offer more, especially to young people who still had the promise of a bright future.

I don't know much about their courtship in Vienna. If they talked about it around me, I was too young to be interested and do not remember any details. But the attraction must have been strong because my father kept in touch with her after they both left Vienna and returned to Poland. After he left, he settled in Lwów, the largest city in western Ukraine and not far from Tarnopol. There my father established a millinery business. In other words, he was a hat maker. In the mid-20th century, almost everyone wore hats as the fashion of the day dictated. Hats were a sign of a person's social and economic status and that made it a lucrative business.

He started the business with one of his cousins, Max Bickel. Their partnership lasted several years as they worked hard to learn the craft. I know almost nothing about Max or what happened to him during the war, but he most certainly perished. I am fortunate to have a photograph of him in which he and my father posed together along with several of their employees for a company photo. Eventually, they also opened up a millinery in Tarnopol and my father moved there. I do not know if they closed the business in Lwów and whether Max moved with him or if they operated two locations. The photograph of them has a plaque with the name of the business and its location was in Tarnopol. But at some point they dissolved their partnership. I never learned the reasons why they parted company or whether it was because they had disagreements. I don't remember my father ever speaking about it. The factory in Tarnopol also had a retail store to sell the hats directly to the public. After he was re-established there, he and my mother married. I do not know anything about how they reconnected or the specifics of the wedding. And even now I cannot remember their anniversary date.

There are so many things I would like to know about their lives before I was born, but the crimes that were committed against us have robbed me of that opportunity. I struggle now to piece together those early days of our lives in Tarnopol. I do remember my father's store was beautiful and elegantly appointed to appeal to many of the well-to-do customers that frequented it. Inside there was a balcony that overlooked the floor of the shop and I recall as a young boy standing on it and watching the gorgeous ladies below who came to buy our hats. It was an exciting place to be during a time of great happiness for our family.

The apartment in which we lived wasn't large or luxurious but it was pleasant and cozy and my mother worked hard to give it a homey feel. I can still remember the address. It was on Ulica Briknera (Briknera Street) number 7. We were on the second floor of the building and each floor had two apartments. Ours had three bedrooms and my parents slept in one room, while my sister slept in another. My brother and I shared the third room. The apartment had a balcony which overlooked the streets of Tarnopol.

My earliest memories are rooted at this home, some of which were very pleasant and some that cause me some embarrassment. One of those pleasant memories was of our next-door neighbors. They had a daughter who was about my age and, even though I was very young, I was already beginning to notice girls. Her name was Nusia and I remember we used to play together and the thrill I got whenever we touched. It was all very innocent, but I can still feel the sensation of touching her backside while she was wearing a satin dress. It is as vivid as if it happened yesterday.

But most of my memories bring back a twinge of embarrassment. When I think of the balcony, I remember an incident which reminds me what a brat I could be. One summer day, my brother and sister were packing and preparing for a camping trip sponsored by a local Jewish youth organization. The camp was only for teenagers, and at the time I was too young to go. I was envious of them and thought it was so unfair that I couldn't go along. I began to insist that I be allowed to go with them. Of course, my parents ignored my unreasonable demand. Crestfallen and angry, I concocted a plan to issue an ultimatum. I ran up to the balcony, climbed up on the railing and pretended to ready myself for a leap from it. Then I turned and said with the most dramatic voice I could muster, "If I don't get to go, I'm going to jump off the balcony!" My brother and sister started laughing uncontrollably. My father, on the other hand, did not find it funny and quickly quieted them with his loud and authoritative voice. I doubt that he thought I would really follow through with my threat, but he was afraid that I might accidentally fall in all the excitement.

That wasn't the only time I showed myself to be an urchin. As the youngest child, I was spoiled and pampered. Misdeeds and misbehaviors were almost a pastime for me and I seldom was punished for them. Once, however, I did something very dangerous, and—rightfully so—I got in big trouble for it. One day, I don't remember why, I got angry at our maid, whose name was Regina, and I started yelling at her. In a fit of rage, I grabbed a kitchen knife and threw it at her. I could have really injured her, but luckily, I wasn't such a good knife thrower and I missed her completely. Needless to say, my parents punished me severely.

On another occasion, my father was planning to travel to Stanisławów to see his parents. I desperately wanted to go with him. But for some reason he didn't want me to come this time. To distract me from the idea, he promised to buy me a toy sword I had been eyeing. The sword came with a belt equipped with a long sheath. I eagerly agreed to the bribe, and he bought me the sword. It was great getting the toy, and for a few days I played it with it, happily contented. But then the day came when it was time for my father to go on his trip. By then the novelty and excitement of the sword had worn off. The thought of missing out on my father's adventure overwhelmed me with disappointment. I began to cry and I pestered my father to take me with him. He resisted, but I refused to let it go. I grew increasingly persistent and obnoxious until finally, he relented.

In today's world, a trip like that wouldn't be in any way considered an adventure; Stanisławów was only 129 kilometers away and a short journey by train. But for a young boy in 1930s Poland it seemed like a great adventure. However, the excitement was short-lived. Although I loved to see my grandparents, once we arrived, I became bored quickly. There were few activities with which to occupy myself, and I didn't have any friends my age in Stanisławów. After only a day or two, I began to miss being at home, and I started to cry and plead with my father to take me back. I feel bad now for the torment I probably caused him as a child—he must have wondered what he had done to raise such a little devil. My brother summed it up well when he once said about me: "My kid brother was a nuisance. He always wanted to tag along. He wanted to do everything I did, but he was five years younger!" I always irritated him with my obstinate persistence.

Certainly, the life of ease I had as a boy contributed to my impudence. It was a wonderful time filled with special memories. We spent our summers in the Carpathian Mountains nearby, something the average family couldn't afford to do. My brother, my sister and I would go with our mother for a month, while our father stayed in Tarnopol and took care of the business. Then, the following month, our father would come to stay with us while our mother would return to the city to take her turn caring for the business.

We traveled to the mountains by train and the journey always filled my siblings and me with excitement. We would hire a *daroshka*, a Polish word for a horse and buggy, to pick us up with our luggage to take us to the train station. I loved to ride up front beside the driver, because sometimes he would let me take the reins.

We didn't own a vacation home, so each year we'd rent a different cabin and stay in a different part of the mountains. A river named the *Prut* ran through the region. With its countless boulders, rapids, and pools it offered us endless activities and adventures along its banks. But one thing I enjoyed most was just quietly sitting by its edge and skipping stones across the water. We went on hikes through the beautiful forest groves and the steep mountain hillsides. My father made friends with those who lived in the area. So it seemed we always had lots of local kids to play with when we visited.

Every once in a while my grandfather would come from nearby Stanisławów to visit us while we were in the mountains. My uncles would also come to visit occasionally. I remember one of our uncles we particularly loved to join us. His name was Haim, and he was younger, closer to our age, and seemed more like a cousin. We spent hours and hours playing soccer with him. We had a nanny who would also come with us to help take care of us all. Her name was Zosia, and she used to take us on all kinds of activities, to the park, picnics, skating and to the movies. She even played ball with us occasionally. Luckily for her, she immigrated to Palestine before the war. I was able to see her when I visited Israel years later.

I have very fond memories of this tranquil and happy period in my life and those wonderful summer days. Then came the summer days of 1939 and there would be no more vacations for a long time. Having just turned eleven years old, the terror to come would accelerate my passage from boyhood to manhood exponentially.

3   DARK CLOUDS OF WAR

The beginning of the war in the late 1930s didn't come as a total surprise to us. Even a cursory glance at the events unfolding in Europe would reveal that war was a great possibility. We read the newspapers and we listened to the radio. We were one of the few in the area who could afford a German-made *Telefunken*. These radios were considered the very best in the world at the time and we could receive broadcasts from all over Europe. Many times, in the years leading up to the war, we heard Hitler's fiery speeches filled with antisemitic remarks. For me as a young boy, all of this news was of little concern. It was from far away and had no impact on my everyday life. But for my father and mother, it gave them reason to worry and created angst. Yet they couldn't imagine the horror that lay ahead for them and our fellow Jews.

As the dark clouds of war grew over Europe and antisemitism spread across the continent, many Jews became nervous, and began to consider their options in the face of the threat. Some with the foresight to anticipate what was to come immigrated to Palestine and others to the United States. In retrospect, it's easy to argue that my family should have seen the signs and that we should have left

Poland like they did. As the old saying goes, hindsight is twenty-twenty. But in the reality of the moment, the situation was very complex and evaluating it not so clear. No one could predict the future in such uncertain times. I'm sure even those who left before the war started didn't fully anticipate the terror that would be unleashed.

For my parents, leaving would have meant abandoning the rewards of years of hard work that had created the comfortable lifestyle we enjoyed. They had spent their adult years building a successful business, raising a family in a comfortable home, and becoming an integral part of the local community. In the face of such great uncertainty, the first choice was not to leave everything behind—even though we were given an opportunity. We had relatives in the United States. My mother's sister, whose name was Lena, had emigrated there sometime in the 1920s, well before the trouble started in Poland. She was diligent to stay in touch with her family and kept a close eye on world news. As events became bleaker, she became deeply concerned about our future. In 1939, she wrote to us and suggested that we come to the United States. She told us that she would help us make the move and to begin to build a new life in this land of opportunity.

But my father knew that Jewish immigrants to the U.S. often led very difficult lives, and that it could be challenging to find well-paying work. He realized that if he were to leave his thriving business for America, his family's lifestyle would change dramatically. And since war wasn't yet a certainty, he felt that it was best for us to stay and see what would happen. Having spent time in Austria he had a great respect for the culture of Germanic people and believed they were the most civilized in the world. And, while he wasn't naïve about the dangers of antisemitism, he couldn't believe it would turn violent. Perhaps his store would be boycotted and we would face racial slurs and verbal assaults, but surely the sophistication of the Germans wouldn't permit much more than that. Needless to say, he grossly underestimated the hatred we would soon face. Of course, my father would later deeply regret his decision. It saddens me immensely that for the few short years he remained alive, he was plagued by tremendous guilt and depression, realizing he missed an opportunity to save his family from an awful fate.

In Poland and Eastern Europe, neither antisemitism nor threats of war were new. It had only been a little over a decade since the Poles, Ukrainians and Soviets had fought over possession of the city of Tarnopol. The border between these three countries had shifted many times before and after World War I. With the turmoil, threats and violence against Jewish people in the region became commonplace. But they had always survived and rebuilt through all the strife and hatred. Little did any of us know how different the next incarnation of antisemitism would be.

Then the infamous day of September 1939 came which ignited full-scale war. I had just turned eleven years old a few weeks before Hitler invaded Poland. Before the invasion, he signed a nonaggression pact with Stalin that split the territory of Poland between Germany and the Soviet Union. Hitler's armies came east and quickly conquered western Poland, while at the same time Stalin's forces marched westward rapidly and took the other half. Tarnopol would fall to the Soviets, so we would escape the all-out persecution by the Nazis for the first two years of the war. The Jews who found themselves living on the western side began to feel the hatred of the Nazis very quickly. The Soviets, on the other hand, had no plans to annihilate us, even though many of them were also antisemitic. Nevertheless, our family's life began to change dramatically—not because we were Jews, but because my father owned a factory and a business. We were capitalists, and for that, the Soviets considered us enemies of the State.

It was a time of great trepidation, confusion and fear. The Russians came into Tarnopol without much resistance, but for a couple of weeks there was violence in the streets. Ukrainian and Polish nationals united to fight against the Russians. Some Jews who felt patriotism for their homeland joined them in that fight. Skirmishes broke out in the city as these nationalists attempted to disrupt the Soviet takeover. I remember sitting in our apartment and hearing shots firing as the conflict spread into the streets. There were snipers on top of the buildings and hidden in the alleyways, waiting to ambush the Russian soldiers patrolling the town. But it wouldn't be long before the Soviets would gain full control. The resistance movements were all but silenced, and many of the Polish and Ukrainian activists were arrested and sent to prison. After that, the violence in the streets quieted and we felt safer. But soon our lives would be turned completely upside down.

4   THE SOVIETS TAKE ALL

One day soon after the invasion, the Soviet authorities came knocking on our factory door. They served us with eviction notices and brought in bureaucrats to take over the business. They seized all our assets and everything became the property of the State. I was too young to remember all the details of this seizure. But I remember sensing my father's despondency at losing everything. He was forced to sweep the floors of the very factory he had built and made into a thriving enterprise, and he was paid very little to do it. He was humiliated and dejected.

Imagine working painstakingly and diligently for many years, putting in long and arduous hours only to have your handiwork stripped entirely from you in a matter of days. Unsurprisingly, in the beginning he sympathized more with the Germans than with the Russians. My father was a Viennese-educated businessman who had fought with the Austrians, the not-so-distant cousins of the Germans. He believed firmly in the free market and private ownership of property and capital. He believed that German culture was one of the most advanced in all of history. And although he was aware of Hitler's hatred and his antisemitic policies, he still maintained faith in German civility and was confident that it would prevail in the end. On the other hand, he knew that if the Soviets gained power, it would be devastating for his business—and he was right. No wonder he called the Soviets 'Ivans!' with great disdain. Now his biases were being confirmed.

For a while we were allowed to remain in our apartment in Tarnopol. But the authorities forced us to share it with some lawyers from Russia who worked for the State. Two of the lawyers were men and one a woman. Our apartment wasn't very large but we had no choice and we made room for them all. Even though we were in very tight quarters we didn't have much social interaction with them. They kept to themselves and we did the same. As awkward as this living arrangement was, they were for the most part pleasant and did not annoy us. However, my brother Edek probably enjoyed it more than any of us. He thought the female attorney was attractive and enjoyed flirting with her. She seemed to enjoy it as well, much to Edek's delight. I'm sure the escapade helped make the uncertain time more tolerable for him.

The time for me was also not spent in complete despair. In fact, in one way I was happier after the Soviets took over than before because of a unique opportunity they gave me. The Soviets were very keen on the arts and culture and encouraged all children to participate. I was able to join a Russian folk-dance group at a center for activities called the Young Pioneers Palace. These were established to develop young people to serve in Soviet system. My teacher was a Jewish woman named Mrs. Orlinski who was a refugee from the Nazi invasion of Warsaw. We learned many different types of traditional Russian folk dances and we performed them on stage in costumes. I practiced hard and became very good at them. As part of the group we were required to wear red scarves to school and for certain events. I also enjoyed singing so I auditioned successfully for a choir group. The group wasn't just for children and its members were mostly adults. I was given solo parts for some of the numbers and was the only child soloist at the time in the choir. The experiences built my confidence, and the thrill of performing on stage in front of hundreds was like nothing I had experienced before.

After the Soviets took over, all citizens were required to get a Soviet passport. On our passports, we were given a designation under a new rule known as 'Paragraph 11.' This meant that we were considered 'bourgeois' and as such we were declared enemies of the State. Since we were viewed as capitalists, the Soviets believed we were a threat to the Communist system. Under Paragraph 11 we were not allowed to live in a city that had a seat of government. Tarnopol was the seat of government for the local county or *Oblast*. Because of this we were eventually forced to leave my hometown.

We asked for permission to move to my mother's childhood town of Tluste, where her parents still lived. The town was only about 100 kilometers away from Tarnopol, but getting there wouldn't be easy. Somehow my father was able to acquire a truck for our move, which made the move much easier. This was actually an amazing feat, since it wasn't easy in those days to obtain access to such a resource. Most people were still using horse and carts to transport big loads. But my father, ever resourceful, found a way to make it happen.

We loaded all the belongings that we could fit onto the truck and my father, mother and I left for Tluste. My brother and sister were allowed to remain in Tarnopol because they were very talented musicians. They too had been given opportunities to study music after the Soviets arrived and had chosen to play the violin. For this reason, they were allowed to continue their studies in the city. They both played with the local orchestra, which was comprised of about 100 members. Although my brother and sister were very young, they were talented enough to be considered an indispensable part of the group. However, not long after, they too were forced to leave. My sister joined us in Tluste, while my brother, whom the Soviets recognized as exceptionally talented, was sent to Czortkow to continue his musical studies. Czortkow was a small town only a little bigger than Tluste, located about halfway between Tarnopol and our new village. When we arrived in Tluste we settled into a small apartment in a building my grandfather owned. My grandparents lived in an adjoining apartment and the bakery that he owned was also a part of the small complex. It was quite a downgrade from our living style in Tarnopol, but it was relatively comfortable and—at least for the time being—it was safe from the tumult engulfing the rest of Europe. My father found a job with a local clothing factory as an accountant, a role for which he was overqualified after having run his own millinery factory for so many years.

I don't feel like I ever really got to know my grandfather. He was a pious Jew and wore a beard with long locks on his sideburns, as did all traditional Jews. My father, on the other hand, wasn't very religious and we were not raised according to orthodoxy. As a result, I found it difficult to identify with my grandfather. He seemed always to be judging me and I fell short of his expectations and approval.

When we lived in Tarnopol, our family did keep many Jewish traditions. We always celebrated the holidays, and on Friday evenings we'd have a Sabbath meal with lighted candles. We'd go to the synagogue on Sabbaths, but not every week. My father appreciated the music and the singing at the temple, but the experience wasn't a deeply religious one for him. He instilled in us a love for the long-held traditions of our ancestors and made sure that we'd carry them forward. We were instilled with the belief that these traditions were important for the survival of the Jewish culture. But once we came to Tluste, we were so focused on survival that we became much less observant.

After the Germans invaded western Poland, many Jews fled eastward choosing to be under Soviet rule rather than suffer the fate that awaited them under the Nazis. Some of them came to Tluste and nearby towns and villages. The influx of fleeing Jews continued to occur even after we arrived there. They relayed terrible stories about the plight of Jews in Warsaw, Krakow, and other Polish cities under German control. But the Soviets didn't allow them all to stay and many of them were sent to Siberia. We were afraid that we would also be forced to go there; especially since we had been identified as capitalists. Could we have been better off had we been exiled there rather than living under the Germans? The impossibility of knowing the best course of action in those difficult times is illustrated by the fate of one of our neighbors from Tluste. They were expelled to Siberia but decided that it would be best if they left their 6-year-old son in Tluste with a family. Ultimately, they survived living in Siberia, but after the war, they returned to find that tragically, their son had died at the hands of the Nazis.

All the stories coming from the refugees from western Poland were terribly frightening to me, but I was still a young boy, and I was ultimately more preoccupied with having fun with my friends. I don't remember my parents ever trying to explain to me what was happening, but I sensed their mounting stress and nervousness as the awful tales and harrowing news from abroad came with increasing frequency.

Like most young boys, I adapted quickly to changes, and my life in Tluste soon came to seem normal. Over time, I began to miss Tarnopol less, and I accepted the fact that our family was now forging a different path toward the future. I became active in school and I became popular among my peers. My prestige grew because of my talent as a folk dancer. I was given opportunities to take the stage and show off the dances I had learned in Tarnopol at the Young Pioneers Palace. My peers were impressed by the acrobatics and gravity-defying moves that characterized those traditional Russian dances. The colorful decorative costumes and the emotionally compelling music added excitement to the routines. In the small town of Tluste, very few had ever seen these dances—much less learned to perform them. I seized the opportunity to show off my skills at my new school, and soon I became somewhat of a celebrity and star of the stage.

In one of my favorite performances, I would lift up my leg in a lithe, acrobatic move, and then suddenly I would pretend to fall as if lightning had stricken me. The audience would gasp and gaze at me with worried looks, concerned for my safety. Then I would slowly pull myself up, still feigning injury but as the music gradually got faster and faster, I would begin to match the rhythm until the song was once again at full speed. Once the audience realized the fall had been part of the routine, their eyes would light up with laughter and amusement. Since I had to make sure my movements were synchronized with the beat, this dance step was almost always improvised.

Soon after I started attending school in Tluste, I met a boy named Sam Langholz. Sam would become a lifelong friend of mine, and we are still close friends today. We were quite different because of our upbringing. He had grown up in Tluste, and his life was a much humbler one than the one I had lived in the bigger city of Tarnopol. I was a soft, cultured and spoiled city boy. He was a typical small-town youngster, not as polished and aware of the bigger world as I, but savvy, hardworking and very practical. In spite of our differences, we became fast friends—perhaps even *because* we were so different. He fascinated me because he had tremendous 'street smarts.'

Throughout our friendship, he showed me how to get along in a world that was less gilded than the one from which I had come. That was of tremendous value to me the rest of my life. I like to think that in return I gave him an awareness of a more cosmopolitan upbringing, sharing the music, art and culture I had encountered during my time in the big city. Sam and I have remained close friends for almost 80 years, even though we took different routes out of Europe to come to America, and then lived on opposite sides of the country.

Sam's father was a tinsmith and metalworker, and I loved to visit his workshop. It was like a playground for me. All of the fascinating tools and workbenches filled me with wonder and curiosity. Sam would take me there and we would play for hours, pretending we were real metal smiths. It was here in this workshop that Sam performed a remarkable feat of heroism, which I will reveal later. His act of unselfishness would be extremely difficult for the bravest of adult men to commit, but considering that he was only a thirteen-year-old boy, his actions were truly phenomenal.

5 THE REAL TERROR BEGINS

In June of 1941, bad news arrived from western Poland. The Germans had launched 'Operation Barbarossa', an attack designed to conquer the rest of Poland, the Baltic States, and eventually Russia. It was in direct violation of the German-Soviet Non-aggression Pact that split Poland between the two powers. Hitler gave the order to send troops eastward, with the intent of conquering Eastern Europe and create *Lebensraum* or 'Living Space' for the German people. The famous offensive would ultimately lead to the Nazi downfall, but for the next few years, it would cause the most horrific consequences for the Jews there.

This news was very unsettling for us. For the many years that Hitler had been in power, we had warily kept abreast of news from Germany. We had the Telefunken radio and we could get stations from all over Europe. My father spoke German very well, so we favored listening to news from Berlin and other German cities. We had heard Hitler's speeches first hand, and his fiery rhetoric astonished us and made us very nervous. And now that the Germans had been in western Poland for almost two years, many reports of what the Nazis were doing to the Jews there had reached us. The stories of the ghetto in Warsaw and the mass deportation of our people to concentration camps came to us frequently. If the Soviets couldn't hold the front, we knew that we would be facing a similar fate soon.

The German forces moved swiftly. The Soviet troops, who by now lacked the proper resources to defend themselves, offered little resistance to the terribly efficient Nazi war machine. In the span of only a few short weeks, the Russians were forced to retreat from the entire region around Tluste. As the troops fled, many Jews decided to go with them rather than suffer at the hands of the Germans. Some of them tried to convince my father to go as well, but he was still suspicious of the 'Ivans' and decided that it would be better to remain in Tluste. Remembering his years spent in Vienna, once again he held firmly to the belief that the Germans were too cultured to commit fatal atrocities. "What is the worst they will do?" he asked. "Maybe they will put a sign over my store that says, 'This is a Jewish store.' That is bad, but I can survive that." On the other hand, the Soviets had confiscated everything he owned—a fate far worse than he believed he would meet at the hands of the Germans.

As the Russians fled eastward, they moved their ammunition by train. Some of those arms came through the Tluste train station. Sometime at the end of June or the beginning of July 1941, the station had a trainload of Soviet ammunition waiting there. The Russians believed they couldn't get the train out before the Germans would be upon them. Rather than leave the ammunition for the Germans to use, they decided to destroy it by blowing up the entire train.

We didn't live far from the railroad station. One day we heard an incredible blast. The ground shook violently underneath us and buildings jolted on their foundations. A massive wave of smoke, ashes and the suffocating smell of sulfur enveloped everything in the town. We could hardly breathe. Everything was covered in the residue from the huge blast. A rumor spread that there was going to be a second explosion soon. So, we grabbed a few things and we made our way to some empty fields outside of the town. For two nights we camped out under the open sky enveloped by the warm summer evening.

It was a nightmare for us, but we had managed to get away from the terrible stench and ashes. Yet as awful as this experience was, there was still time to be a young boy and to experience the wonderful things in life. While we were camped in the tall grass and under a roof made up of millions of brilliant stars, my heart turned to the thrill of young love.

Camping next to us just happened to be the family of a young girl from my school on whom I had a boyhood crush. In the midst of this frightening event, my heart found joy at being so close to her. I remember she wore a beautiful, yellow flowered dress that shone in the summer sun and enticed me to flirt with her unendingly. I did everything I could to get her attention and impress her during those two short days on our 'camping trip.' But soon there would be no time for pursuing puppy love. In fact, there would be no time for anything but survival.

As the Soviets fled, Hungarian troops followed them and reached Tluste ahead of the Germans. They were allied with Germany and came to support the offensive. Ukrainian nationalist groups began to rally together in the hopes of declaring an independent Ukraine in the ensuing vacuum of power. Under Russian rule, many of them had been branded enemies of the state, and they were eager to seek retribution and oust their oppressors. Some of their leaders, anticipating the Soviet retreat, declared Ukraine an independent country even before the Soviets had left Tluste. The nationalists had a sizable base in the village, and many of them were as antisemitic as the Nazis.

A few of our former Gentile neighbors still treated us with respect, and did what they could to help us as our situation grew worse. But ultimately our former friends and associates were powerless, and if they were suspected of collaborating with Jews, they could face grave consequences. But mostly the local Poles and Ukrainians were happy to see our fate at the hands of the Nazis. They too wanted to see all Jews eradicated.

Once the Germans finally arrived, they enlisted the locals to help them determine who was Jewish. The Polish and Ukrainians always knew the identities of Jews, even if they didn't look Jewish; after all, it is hard to keep one's identity secret in a small village like Tluste. Most of the villagers were eager to help, and wouldn't have hesitated to expose a Jew found hiding.

But beyond simply informing on Jews, many of these locals themselves initiated violence against Jews, knowing that the approaching Germans were ready to begin the process. That June, a mob of Ukrainians arrived in a nearby village and began killing any Jews they met. These locals were delighted to hear that the Germans were advancing, and they seized the opportunity to act upon their festering hatred. They hunted down their Jewish neighbors and proceeded to kill them in savage and brutal ways: they stabbed them with pitchforks, hacked them with axes and brutally beat them with shovels and hammers.

Word spread quickly of the incident along with the rumor that they would soon come to Tluste since there was a large Jewish population there. The people began to panic, but upon hearing the news, two priests from Tluste, one a Ukrainian Greek Orthodox and the other a Polish Catholic, bravely set out to confront the people and stop the pogrom.

The priests encountered the mob on the main road to Tluste not far from the town limits. The crowd halted to listen to what the priests had to say. Instead of appealing to the would-be murderers' sense of love or mercy, the priests played upon their fear. They asked the crowd, "Why would you sully your hands with blood when the Germans will do it for you?" Then they admonished them, saying, "Don't let this sin stain your hands. Let Hitler do the dirty work for you." It is impossible to know whether these priests actually cared about our fate as Jews, but their actions showed a measure of compassion and dignity for which the rattled townsfolk were grateful.

Indeed, Hitler's troops would be on our doorstep soon. Within weeks they would be in full control of Tluste, just as I marked my thirteenth birthday. For me, there was nothing to celebrate about finally becoming a teenager.

6   THE GERMANS COME TO TLUSTE FOR THE FIRST TIME

The German forces approached Tluste from the west and the south as they pursued the fleeing Soviet troops. It was an ominous sight as the victorious forces began to move through our little town. I remember seeing the stern and intimidating faces of German officers as they rode in their open-top automobiles, dressed impeccably in drab, grey, medal-draped uniforms. The ground shook and rumbled nervously as the big lumbering trucks rolled down the main street, their beds packed end to end and side to side with nameless and faceless gun-wielding soldiers ready to disembark and engage the enemy at a second's notice. They moved together in unison, as though a single monstrous organism had come to devour its prey.

The fear and dread they inspired at that moment was nothing compared to the reality of the horror they would eventually bring. As frightened as we were at their coming, we still had no idea what these human-shaped instruments of death were fully capable of inflicting. But we were soon to find out.

The major fighting units kept moving toward the shrinking border of the Soviet Union. A small outfit was left behind to establish order and to begin to implement the new rules of the Third Reich. Before long, Jews would no longer be free to come and go as they pleased. We would be forced to wear the armbands that the Nazis used to identify Jews. More rumors continued to circulate of Jews being murdered and their homes looted by the locals in neighboring towns. We knew now that our future was bleak, but it was too late for us to flee amid all the chaos the front lines of war had brought.

In a few days, more Hungarian forces arrived in Tluste. But they didn't come to fight. Instead, they were bringing Jews who were being expelled from Hungary. Many of these Jews had fled to Hungary from the west as rumors of the war began to fly. Once the war started, the flow of Jews from Poland and other parts of Eastern Europe into that country increased. The Hungarian officials began to target these people and dedicated significant resources to getting them out. At first, the deportation was slow and difficult, but after the Germans drove out the Soviets from Galicia, the Hungarians were permitted by the German authorities to bring Jews there. Tens of thousands of Jews were brought into the region and wound up in the ghettos all over the area surrounding Tluste.

When the Germans came, everything that resembled normalcy in our lives ended. In August they appointed a military governor of Tluste and the systematic reign of terror in our little town began. A new police force was commissioned and staffed mostly by the local Ukrainians. The Germans were now fully in control, assisted by the antisemitic locals.

Soon after, the German officials established a *Judenrat* in Tluste as they had done in all other occupied regions. This was a committee or council of Jews assigned by the Nazis to act as a liaison between the Nazi officials and the Jewish people. Their job was to help the Nazis enforce the laws imposed upon the Jews. They were also forced to extort money and valuables from the Jewish community, help round up Jews for work in the labor camps and even sometimes to deliver them for execution.

One of the first rules the Judenrat had to help enforce was a method the Nazis devised so that Jews could always be immediately identified. We were made to wear armbands at all times while we were in public. My mother had to make ours. She sewed together a white cloth with the blue Star of David. Later curfews were established, and all Jews were forced to live in a particular section of the town. These restricted areas famously became known as 'ghettos.' Every city under Nazi occupation had one. Of course, the one in Warsaw was probably the largest and most notorious, and walls and fences confined it. In Tluste they didn't wall us in, so we were not as confined, but we were still to remain in our section at all times.

Once these rules were in place, life quickly became a monumental struggle. We could no longer go shopping, even for basic necessities, as we were banned from entering any stores. It became challenging to get the food we needed. One had to have a connection with a 'Gentile' and have something to exchange in order to get food. A lot of people were starving, especially the poorer people. Jewish children were no longer allowed to attend school, and Jewish doctors and lawyers were ordered to stop their practices. We were forbidden to socialize with Christians.

7 A FEARED ANTI-SEMITE RETURNS TO TLUSTE

Earlier in the 1930s, as rumors of war had begun to spread across Europe, antisemitism started its ugly rise in popularity and acceptance. Attacks against Jewish people both violent and non-violent had begun to increase. Jews in every city, town and village across Poland experienced verbal taunting, vandalism of personal property and outright assaults. Bigotry and racism were on open display like never before. Poles and Ukrainians made Jews the scapegoats for every perceived societal or economic ill. We had faced this tide of hatred in Tarnopol during the few years leading up to the war. antisemites organized protests and boycotts at my father's factory and shop. Groups of ultra-right-wing students gathered in front of our business and taunted any who tried to patronize us. They were effective to some degree in damaging our business and income. Those were frightening times as we began to realize the storm that was gathering on the horizon.

The Jews in Tluste had faced the same troubles leading up to the outbreak of war. For many years before we moved there, some of the Ukrainians and Poles in the village actively bullied and terrorized them. The incidents didn't occur often and the majority of the people in the town didn't participate, but there were some who seemed to enjoy it like it was a hobby or a sport.

One man in particular was notorious among the Jews, and he created his fair share of trouble. His name was Hryzei Timush and he was a hardened antisemite. He had become known to almost everyone simply as Timush. The best word to describe him was 'hooligan,' and the very sound of his name invoked fear. The Jews there often said that he couldn't go to bed at night without causing some fear or despair for the local Jewish people. He broke the windows of Jewish shops and homes as he stumbled home late in the evening, drunk from his visit to a local pub. Another of his cruel pastimes was to catch a local orthodox Jew by his long beard and attempt to cut it off. He was an evil character and a dangerous nuisance. All the Jews in Tluste did their best to avoid him.

Timush was also an adamant Ukrainian Nationalist. Ukrainians had been hoping and yearning for an independent Ukraine for hundreds of years. While the turmoil on the world scene caused anxiety and fear for most of the world, many Ukrainians were optimistic that another European conflict might bring an opportunity for a free and independent state for them—something that had never been accomplished even though they had fought for it at various times against all the surrounding nationalities for many centuries.

Once the Russians arrived in Poland, they began to search out and arrest anyone who posed a threat to the Soviet regime. Among those were Ukrainian Nationalists. Nationalism of any kind was considered a dangerous enemy of the Soviet's goal of expanding their empire. Well before we arrived in Tluste, they had already captured and sent to prison hundreds of these Nationalists. Among them was Timush.

We are pretty certain that someone in Tluste denounced Timush to the Soviet secret police. That unit was known then as the

NKVD, an acronym for the Russian words that meant 'The People's Commission for Internal Affairs.' The NKVD was the forerunner of the notorious Soviet spy organization, the KGB, and was given far-reaching authority for all police matters. The organization often operated completely independent with little oversight from any other governmental agency. It conducted executions without trials, deported mass populations perceived as threats to the Soviet government and mass executions of political prisoners.

Once Timush had been denounced, the NKVD came for him quickly and raided his home. They found in his house some anti-Soviet literature and several guns. He was arrested immediately, given a shoddy trial in a kangaroo-like court and condemned to execution for treason. He was sent to a prison in Berdichev, a town about 300 kilometers northeast of Tluste. Here he waited on death row for months, fearful and dejected, and contemplated his shortened life.

In prison, he was placed in a cell next to an Orthodox priest who had also been condemned to death by the Soviets. We never found out who this priest was, where he was from, or why he was imprisoned. The Soviets never officially outlawed any religions, but the State's ultimate goal was to eradicate religion. As a result, they often targeted the religious leadership, especially if their influence was too significant in the community.

Timush and the priest couldn't see each other, but they could hear one another. So, they talked frequently and became close friends. Timush, being Christian, slowly revealed his life story to this priest, and began to confess his sins. He told the priest about his violent past and the persecution he had inflicted on the local Jews in his hometown. The priest admonished Timush for his deep-seated hatred and bigotry and told him he must repent of his crimes. Humbly, Timush agreed as he prepared for his death and the unknown of what would come for him afterward.

The priest, with little hope or optimism, counseled Timush that if he—by some astonishing miracle—were to escape the prison and his inevitable death, he must atone for his violent acts. Timush, perhaps in great anticipation that such a miracle could occur, exuberantly promised that he would. He vowed then and there never to hurt a living thing ever again. He wouldn't harm the smallest of animals, a bee, a fly, the tiniest flower and not even a Jew. It seemed that Timush's repentance was sincere, but was it too late?

In the first week of July, the Soviets began to flee Berdichev and, as they had done in every other city as they evacuated, they executed thousands of prisoners. Rather than allow their political prisoners to survive and join forces against them later with the Nazis, the Russians decided to eradicate them. Timush was certain that his death would be coming soon. He waited alongside his new priest friend for their number to be called to be taken to a firing squad.

As the German war machine advanced eastward past Tluste, it quickly came to the city of Berdichev. Ahead of the occupation of these towns and cities, the *Luftwaffe*, or the German air force, pounded the targets with massive bombings. One day the air raids started, and Timush sat fearfully in his cell as everything around him shook violently. He most likely prayed along with the priest knowing that any minute their lives could end.

Suddenly a gigantic explosion rocked the prison building. A German bomb had struck the prison. Screams and shouts could be heard everywhere as the prisoners were being buried alive in the rubble. Timush's ears were now pounding with the pain from the loud blast of the explosion. His eyes were filled with dirt and dust as the walls of his cell collapsed. He waited for the commotion to settle and wondered if he was still alive. He cleared the debris from his eyes and looked around. One wall of his cell was gone entirely and beams of sunlight pierced through the dust in the air.

He was still breathing. He had survived the blast. But few others in the prison had been so fortunate, including the priest. He lay motionless under the rubble. Timush couldn't waste another second. He pulled himself up and darted toward the newly created opening. He was free! The miracle that neither he nor the priest believed could happen had indeed occurred.

News of Timush's escape took only a few days to reach Tluste. He would be returning soon to his hometown. Fear and dread gripped the Jews when they found out. No one yet knew of his encounter with the priest in prison. They were only aware of his astonishing escape from death row. What evil and terror would he bring with him? If he suspected he had been denounced, whom would he blame? Would he not think a Jew had turned him in? How would he seek revenge? If he had been so vicious before this, what level of cruelty would he rise to after such a fate?

Stories of his taunting, vandalism and violence against Jews before his imprisonment were rife, and the fear rose to panic. No one doubted that he would instigate a pogrom and incite a killing spree. Indeed, the local Ukrainians had already shown they were ready and willing to participate in such activities. There was no way for any of us to flee. We were confined to the ghetto and leaving would have meant certain death. People began burying all their money and valuables. They created hiding places in attics, basements, behind walls and underneath floorboards. But ultimately everyone knew that escape from this monster would be nearly impossible. All we could do was wait now, hoping and praying for some kind of miracle. Little did we know that one had already occurred.

Timush eventually arrived in Tluste. We were sure that any day now an *akcia* would start, led by Timush and his Ukrainian colleagues. An *akcia* was, in essence, a 'pogrom' or a raid in which an order would go out from the Nazis to form an organized attack to round up Jews and bring them for imprisonment or execution. The local Ukrainians and Poles were expected to assist and join the hunt to find and corral the victims. Sometimes the Judenrat and the Jewish ghetto police also were forced to help. But all was quiet. Nothing happened for weeks. The panic died down and the fear lessened. But we were still on tenterhooks, not sure if or when he would unleash his terror.

A couple of months later my sister, Tusia, and my aunt, Bela, were forced to go to work in a nearby villa that once belonged to Jews, but had been taken over by the Germans after their occupation. Their job was to help clean it. One Sunday afternoon they were working together beating out the dirt from rugs just outside the office of the villa, when along came a very nice-looking man—handsomely dressed in a finely tailored blue suit and a well-made hat. The man had come there to find people he could hire to help with some work he needed to be done.

As he neared the office door, he turned toward the two women and his expression lit up as a smile slowly came over his face. He recognized my aunt from his days before his imprisonment. He started toward them to speak to them. My aunt was fearful because she didn't know what to expect from this man who had terrorized them years before. As he approached, he began to very politely ask how Bella was doing. Bella answered with a short reply in hopes the conversation wouldn't last too long. Then the man turned toward Tusia, but still speaking to Bella said, "You I remember, but I don't recognize this lady." Bella replied, "Oh! This is my niece Tusia from Tarnopol." He very graciously introduced himself to her giving his name. But Tusia, sensing Bella's trepidation at seeing him, was so nervous about the encounter that she forgot his name no sooner than he had spoken it.

As soon as he entered the office and the door closed behind him, Tusia looked over at Bella. Her face had turned white with fear. Tusia anxiously asked her what the matter was. Bella's voice trembled as she spoke, "Do you know who that man is? He is Timush!" Tusia replied, "This is Timush?! The man who is going to kill all the Jews in town? He looks very decent and nice." Bella answered quickly and firmly, "He looks decent, but he's not."

When the man returned from the office, he came over to them again and he looked at Tusia and with sincere empathy said, "I am so sorry you have to do work like this. You look like you should be sitting in a living room playing the piano." Both women were stunned by his gentle words and graciousness.

When Tusia returned home that night, she couldn't wait to tell us about this encounter with the most feared man in Tluste. She insisted that he had seemed like such a nice man. She couldn't believe he was capable of the kind of trouble for which he had become known. We knew that Tusia wouldn't invent such a story and her optimism upon meeting Timush gave us a glimmer of hope. But we were still not reassured that we were safe from the man who had wrought such terror. So we continued to be on guard and expect the worst.

8 NEAR DEATH FOR EDEK

In November 1941, word went out that all healthy Jewish men were to report to the German authorities to be taken to a forced labor camp. The order was given by the German authorities but carried out by the Judenrat. Initially, these workers were labeled as 'volunteers,' but everyone knew that anyone who did not 'volunteer' would suffer dire consequences.

I was too young to go, but my brother was put on the list of local men who were old enough and able-bodied to work. It was made clear to us that if he did not report, there would be retribution against our entire family. My brother was scared and my parents didn't want him to go because they knew conditions in these camps were horrible. But very bravely Edek insisted on going to save the rest of us from being terrorized or killed by the German and Ukrainian authorities. I remember my father said to my brother, "Please don't go." And my brother said, "If I don't go, the family will suffer. There will be serious consequences since I am already on the list of those who must go to work." With fearful tears, my father had to agree there was no other way.

The day for him to report came on November 15. I remember the day very well. It was a very cold and dark day even though winter wasn't officially here. The symbolism of that wasn't lost on me as we realized we might never see him again. I remember embracing him and saying goodbye. My mother gave him some clothing and fervently kissed and hugged him. One by one we all said our farewells and then he joined the other men in town to begin their long march to the town of Czortkow. Among the others was our uncle, Hersh Rosenblatt, who was married to my mother's sister, Bronia. There they were put on the train that would take them to the labor camp.

The work camp was near a small town named Kamionki. It was a forced labor camp, but ultimately its purpose was to exterminate the laborers brought there. But these 'volunteers', as the Nazis had falsely proclaimed them, were going to be doing useful work. They were primarily quarrying and crushing rock for the building of roads. But already rumors of what was really happening at these camps had reached us. We had heard that the workers didn't last long under the cruel conditions. They were fed just as little as possible to keep them working. They were not adequately housed from the elements, clothed or cared for medically. The prisoners were literally being worked to death at the lowest possible cost and trouble for the German war machine. What little food they were given was horrible, with almost no nutritional value. Watered down soups and porridges and moldy, stale bread were the norm. Their clothing became tattered and worn with holes and was never washed or repaired. Scurvy, lice and disease spread everywhere to everyone.

As I pointed out in the description of our better days, before the war in Tarnopol, we had lived a very pampered life. My brother, being the son of a successful merchant, never worked very hard physically. So, we knew that he probably wouldn't live long in such excruciating, dismal and squalid work and living conditions. My mother's brother-in-law, her sister's husband was also on the list of 'volunteers' and was at the same camp. They tried to help each other stay alive, but the conditions were so terrible that they both deteriorated rapidly.

The camp was part of the forced labor camp system of the SS, the infamous terror inflicting police force in Nazi Germany. The ultimate goal of the SS was to rid Germany and the rest of Europe of the Jewish people. So, these camps, in reality, became extermination camps. The people brought to them were used to accomplish needed work to support the German war effort but with the coldly calculated goal of killing the laborers in the process.

Conditions in them were horrific. Prisoners were forced to work long days doing the most exhaustive tasks. They were not given adequate clothing even in the coldest weather. They were fed very little, and there was no attempt to prevent diseases. In fact, all of these conditions were allowed as part of the method for exterminating the Jewish prisoners. The evil masterminds of this system calculated that there would be enough Jews to keep the flow of laborers processed through the camps to accomplish the work needed. The Nazis saw the victims as just a natural resource that could be expended like logs on a fire or gasoline in an engine.

My brother arrived in this camp and it wasn't long before he realized he probably wouldn't return from it. Edek's camp was assigned to build roads under the direction of a private German engineering company hired by the government. He was put to work in a stone quarry 15 kilometers from the camp where they broke up the rocks into gravel. The prisoners were forced to walk to and from the camp every day in freezing weather. They didn't have proper shoes or clothing for such cold conditions.

They were fed only 20 grams of bread a day along with a watered-down soup with a tiny portion of some kind of vegetable, usually potato or leek. Naturally, over time, the prisoners became so weak they could hardly make the walk to the quarry much less do much work breaking up the rocks. At that point, many were shot on the spot, as they were no longer useful to the work effort. Others got so tired, especially on the march to and from the camp, that they would sit down to rest or relieve themselves and couldn't get back up. Many of them froze to death in the spot where they sat or lay down. Once my brother was marching back to camp and he had become extremely thirsty from the long day of labor and the march to and from the quarry. There was no water being offered to the prisoners. Edek saw a large patch of snow in a field alongside the road. His throat was so parched that he could no longer stand it. Taking a great risk, he left the line of prisoners and walked into the field and grabbed a handful of snow and started to eat it. Just as he put it to his lips, he was struck across his back by one of the Ukrainian policemen that guarded over them. He fell to the ground in immense pain and before he could get to his feet again, the policeman kicked him swiftly in the ribs sending him back down to the cold, hard ground. Some of the other prisoners came over to him and pulled him back up before the policeman could continue his assault. They quickly helped him back into the line and the policeman gave up his sadistic attack.

The prisoners were slowly being turned into *Muselmänner*, a slang term that emerged from these camps to describe those who became quite literally only skin and bones because of the starvation and exhaustion. These people often gave up on life at this point collapsed to the ground and slumped over into a prayer-like position. Some scholars believe this is where the slang term came from, as the word derives from the German word for Muslim and these victims were in a position that looked similar to one a Muslim would assume in prayer.

The survival rate in camps like the one at Kamionki was the same as the larger and more notorious 'death camps' such as Auschwitz. People were dying or being killed every day all around my brother.

Aside from the starvation, many were shot on sight for the slightest infraction of the rules. And just as fast as they carried out the dead, new prisoners arrived to replace them, serving their own death sentences. The average person taken to these camps only lived about six weeks.

We began to get more news about these camps and even some about Kamionki where Edek was imprisoned. We knew that there was little time for him and desperately sought for a way to rescue him and Uncle Hersh. We found out from some of the leaders of the local Judenrat that the guards at these camps could be bribed and might sometimes free a prisoner for the right ransom. We were told that the going rate was about $20,000.

My father and mother still had some money and a few valuables. So, they began to sell her jewelry, some fine English linen fabric, leather skins and silver tableware. In the meantime, my mother decided to travel to the camp to make sure that she could find someone there who would be willing to help free them. Notably, she sought the help of what is known in Yiddish as a *macher*. This person was usually Jewish, perhaps a member of the local Judenrat, who could find the person to be bribed and negotiate the deal for such a release.

Focused and determined, she made her plan to go to the camp. She was able to get a horse and buggy driver to take her on the two-and-a-half-day trip to the camp. The weather was dreadfully cold and the journey was difficult, but my mother braved it and arrived at the camp. Once there she approached the gate and spoke to the guard. My brother remembered that day well and was surprised when another prisoner came to him to tell him there was a woman at the gate to see him.

I can only imagine the tears that flowed from them both when they first saw each other through the barbed wire. My brother was so frail he could hardly stand. His skin was pale and ashen. His head was completely shaved and he had bruises, cuts and lesions all over his body. As much as my mother longed to see him again, the sight of him must have horrified her tremendously. No doubt her tears of joy were mixed with tears of fear and despair. Edek was so weak he could hardly speak. All he could manage to get out in words was, "Please! Help me, mother!" |

Now she was even more determined to get them both out. Within a day, she was able to find her macher and arranged to return as soon as possible to finalize the deal. She hurriedly made her way back to Tluste and joined us in our task of selling our valuables. Within a few days, with everything they had sold, added to the money they still possessed, they had enough to complete the bribe. She wasted no time in setting out once again for Kamionki. This time the journey seemed even colder because the roads were covered deep with snow. Instead of a horse and buggy, she hired a horse-drawn sleigh to get her back to the camp.

A few days later Edek was sitting in the camp when a German soldier approached him. He motioned to Edek and said in a forceful tone, "Come with me now!" Edek was at first frightened because he thought he might be executed in the same manner as he had seen so many of his fellow inmates die. But as they moved closer to the gate, he saw our mother there along with Uncle Hersh, and his heart leapt. Could it be that he was about to be given his freedom?

When they reached the gate, the guard quickly and discreetly opened it. As he shoved Edek and Hersh through it into the arms of my mother, he said fiercely, "Now get out of here! But don't ever tell anyone that you were here, what you saw or what you did here!"

My mother and brother needed no more encouragement to flee as fast as they could from that hellish place. They jumped into the sleigh and retreated down the road toward Tluste. Edek was already so sickly that my mother worked hard on the long journey back to keep him warm and as comfortable as possible. Fortunately, she had brought her fur coat with her to keep him covered and safe from freezing to death. Once they were on the way, she realized he was covered in lice and that all that was left of him was skin and bone.

When they finally arrived back at our house, my mother wasted no time in cleaning him up. She got out our largest washtub, filled it with hot water and immersed him in it. She cleaned and dried him thoroughly and then fetched some kerosene. She poured it all over his head and body and wiped him all over. This was the only method for killing the lice that we had available. It must have burned his skin, especially where the cuts and abrasions had been. But I don't remember my brother crying out in pain or complaining in the least. He was so relieved to be home, and the minor sting from a kerosene burn would have been nothing compared to the torture inflicted upon him in the camp.

A few days later, after Edek had recovered somewhat from the trauma, our father came to him and said, "Come with me Edek." As they stood outside together, our father reached into his pocket and pulled out a pack of cigarettes. He opened it and drew out one of them, raising it to place between Edek's lips. Then he took out a match and struck it. The flame lit up both of their faces and as Edek sucked in his breath, the tip of the cigarette began to glow.

They looked at each other, Edek with surprise in his eyes, my father with a half-smile. Edek puffed out the smoke, still wondering. You see, before the war my father had prohibited all of us from smoking, realizing the health dangers. But Edek had always wanted to be like his friends who, in his view, were being treated as adults because they could make their own decision to smoke. Now, my father looked him in the eyes and softly said, "It is OK. You are now a man!"

9 GIVE UP YOUR FURS OR DIE

When my mother arrived, we were all so joyous that she had returned safely with my brother. If there was ever such thing as a miracle, we had undoubtedly witnessed one with Edek's escape and return. So many things could have gone wrong, leading to his or my mother's death. But things were still very bad for us, so the celebration was short lived as we turned once again to the quest for survival.

We were sad and frightened that we had to tell our mother about a new edict that had come down from the Nazis while she was away. They had ordered that all Jews must turn over their radios, gold, silver and any other valuables. Included on the list were furs. My mother prized her fur coat immensely and it had helped get Edek back home from the camp through the frigid weather. But apart from having to give away a much-valued possession, the deadline for turning these items to the authorities had passed while she was gone. We were terribly afraid and didn't know what to do. If we went to turn the fur in now, would we be punished—or worse killed—for failing to meet the deadline? But if we kept it, would we be found out and still suffer the same fate? Many of the locals would remember that my mother owned the fur coat and perhaps some had even seen her returning in it from Kamionki. We felt almost certain that we would be discovered, and our fear grew as we pondered what to do with the coat.

Not only did we fear the retribution for not abiding by the edict, but we were also facing starvation because we had little money and few valuables left to trade for food. Yet the fur coat was still with us. Could we trade it to someone for a little more to eat? It would be a great risk to try, especially considering we had violated the order to turn it in. But which would be worse—dying at the hands of the Nazis or dying of starvation? It wasn't an easy decision, but in the end we decided to seek out someone to trade it to.

Through some contacts in the Judenrat, we found out that there was a Ukrainian who was secretly negotiating trades like this between Jews and the locals. We arranged a meeting to show him the fur and he said that he was pretty sure he had a customer for it. The following Sunday, the man came to us with his clients. When they arrived at our house and opened the door, Tusia's face dropped in surprise and horror. She had recognized the two people who the Ukrainian had brought to buy the coat. She turned to my mother and whispered, "Oh my, this is Timush!"

None of the rest of us had seen him before, but Tusia would never forget the face she had met at the villa months before. Wasting no time, they pulled the Ukrainian man aside who had arranged the deal. With fear and alarm, they told him, "You have killed us! This is Timush! He will take the fur and then denounce us to the Gestapo!" But the man put his hand on my father's shoulder and said, "No. Don't worry. He will not do anything like that." But my parents were not convinced and moved away quickly to talk. They discussed their options quickly and quietly. Remembering the stories of this man and the terror he could commit; they knew what they must do. Suddenly, Timush asked what they wanted as a price for the fur. My mother quickly replied, "Please. You can have it. Just take it for nothing."

Surprised but delighted Timush picked up the coat, turned it around gazing upon it and then helped his wife put it on. It fit perfectly and Timush's wife exclaimed, "I love it. It is so beautiful and comfortable." Timush turned to us and said, "You must want something for it. Please tell me how much." My mother replied, "You can have it, but if you feel like giving us something, then give whatever you think."

Timush and his wife stood silently in disbelief. And then my mother once again broke the silence. "We are city people and have not been living here long. It has been very difficult for us to get food."

After that Timush seemed intrigued by the fact that we had come from a bigger city. He began to ask a lot of questions about where we had come from and what we did before we arrived in Tluste. He and his wife sat down with my parents at the table and they began a long conversation. We could see that he was taken by my mother and father and their experience living a prosperous and cultured life.

Timush had lived all of his life in Tluste. He was a simple man but very intelligent. He was a mechanic by trade and worked in the local mill. He had never been to college or university. But he loved to learn about philosophy, culture and the arts. He saw in my father a person who could teach him about many things that had eluded him living in a small town and not having been educated in a university.

The four of them talked for hours until it was getting very late. Timush and his wife thanked my parents for the coat and the stimulating conversation. Then they rose from the table and said goodbye. They turned and shut the door behind them. Nothing more was said about payment for the fur that night. We were disappointed that we were not going to receive anything for it since we were so hungry. But we were all greatly relieved that we were rid of the fur and safe from any consequences for not turning it in.

One week later, we were sitting quietly in our house. Suddenly there was an unexpected knock on the door. We glanced out of the window and saw Timush standing there. He was stooping under the weight of some bags he was carrying. What could he want? We were surprised but frightened. What was he bringing? So many questions entered our minds amidst the uncertainty and suspicion. We slowly opened the door and Timush enthusiastically greeted us with a broad smile on his face. He pushed through the door dragging the heavy sacks. He moved to the table in the center of the room and plopped them down with a thud. One of the bags opened up at the top and three or four potatoes tumbled out. The other bag hit the table and a puff of white dust billowed up from it.

Timush announced happily, "Here are a few things I have brought you to help feed the family." He pulled back the top and inside we saw potatoes and a full sack of flour!

Even though Timush had never offered anything for the fur coat, he had now returned to bring us the thing we needed more than money or gold. We were so happy to see the rations and relieved that he had come to help and not bring persecution. We couldn't believe our eyes. Had this man really changed? Was he no longer a Jew hater? Was this most feared man among the Jews now trying to help? It was too much to fully process, especially in view of the reality we were beginning to face as the Nazis clamped down on us all around.

After Timush brought the flour and potatoes, he beckoned my father and mother to once again sit at the table and talk. We were beginning to realize that he genuinely was changed and that he was eager to learn from my parents all about the bigger world. He wanted to know what they thought about everything, from politics to religion to the arts and culture. This conversation, like the earlier one when he took the fur coat, would go well into the evening. Their words were passionate and intense as they traded thoughts and ideas. They all enjoyed it very much and soon this would become a weekly ritual. Timush would bring what he could for us to keep us alive, and in return my mother and father would offer their experience and wisdom to this most unlikely new friend.

10 TUSIA'S CLOSE CALL WITH AN SS OFFICER

The end of the year was upon us and the locals had finished their Christmas celebrations. Word came to the ghetto that the local SS officers were planning a New Year's Eve celebration at a nearby villa. One of the members of the Judenrat told us that he was ordered to find three or four young Jewish women to serve at the party. He had been told to make sure they were hard working, efficient and, most importantly, very pretty. He thought Tusia would be perfect for the job and asked for her to work the event. My parents were petrified at the thought of his request, especially after hearing the requirement that the women be good looking. They had heard many stories of Jewish women being taken away to work in brothels catering to the German and Nazi soldiers. Would Tusia fall to this fate if she agreed to go?

The Judenrat official assured them that he would be with the girls at the party and do everything he could to prevent that from happening. He was confident that the SS officers had no intentions to force the women into prostitution. My parents had little power to resist the request so they reluctantly agreed to let her go.

When the night of the party finally came, the Judenrat elder came to escort Tusia to the villa. When they arrived, he offered to take her coat and she complied. After it was off, Tusia realized that the armband identifying her as a Jew was on the arm of the coat. She said to the man, "Oh, I must get the armband and put it on my shirt sleeve." But the man said, "Don't worry about that. You won't need it here." Tusia relented and didn't think about it again.

A few hours into the party, a young SS officer saw Tusia and approached her to ask for a dance. She was shocked and didn't know how to answer. Sensing her hesitation, the officer reached out and grabbed her hand and pulled her onto the dance floor. They danced through a lively waltz and the man seemed to enjoy it immensely. When the song ended, he bowed to her, kissed her hand gently and thanked her for the dance. Still reeling from the fear of what might come of this unexpected event, Tusia quickly returned to the kitchen and out of sight from the partygoers.

Unknown to Tusia or the SS officer, a young Polish girl who had her eye on the soldier, had jealously watched the two of them dancing together. A few minutes later she approached the SS man and whispered something into his ear. Suddenly he stood up straight and a look of rage came over his face. The girl knew who Tusia was and had revealed to the soldier that she was Jewish.

The SS man stomped off into the kitchen to find Tusia and within seconds he was standing in front of her with a fiery red face. He shook his finger at her and shouted, "Are you a Jewess?" Tusia sheepishly answered yes. Suddenly he lunged toward her to grab her, but just as he did another man at the party, who had followed him into the kitchen, stepped in between them and tried to calm him down.

Tusia recognized the man intervening as a local man for whom she had worked on a previous occasion. The man motioned to her to get out. Without any hesitation Tusia fled the kitchen and found the Judenrat official who had brought her there. They both then ran from the room and up into the attic of the house to hide. They waited silently behind some furniture as the SS official continued to scream out over and over, "She didn't tell me she was Jewish! I will find that Jewess and I will kill her!" A few minutes went by and then shots rang out. The officer had pulled his gun and was firing indiscriminately in his ever-increasing rage.

A little while passed and finally the commotion settled down. But every now and then they could hear the officer raising his voice and vowing to kill Tusia. They were in the attic for several hours before they decided it was safe to try to get out of the villa. Quietly they snuck down the stairs, and found a back exit. As they fled into the night, two guards outside the house spotted them and cried out, "Halt! Halt!" One of the guards recognized the Jewish elder as a Judenrat official and knew he was working the party. The sudden recognition put him at ease and he lowered his rifle. Then he called out to them, "Bring us some whiskey when you get a chance!" The elder agreed to the request and he and Tusia walked away as fast as they could.

The Judenrat member could only escort Tusia so far, since he had to return to the party to finish his duties. Now she was all by herself without her armband, which had been left on her coat at the party. She knew she needed to get out of the streets as soon as possible. The closest place was her boyfriend Mendel's house, so she hurried there. Fortunately, she made it without being noticed, and was able to stay until morning.

Mendel's last name was Weinstock and he had grown up in the town of Tluste. I do not know how he and my sister met but he was much older than her. He worked at the local movie theatre and operated the projector there. Mendel was a very handsome man, stylish and always impeccably dressed. He was well liked and highly regarded by most everyone in Tluste. Tusia hid at his home for the entire night and waited nervously, fully anticipating the SS officer to finally find her. But the next day there was no sign of him so she returned home. Fortunately, she never heard from or saw him again.

11 TIME TO HIDE

Timush continued to come week after week, and his friendship with my parents soon grew. The food he brought was a lifesaver, but he went further than that to save our lives. He now took it upon himself to keep a constant ear out, listening for news of any kind related to one of our most feared words: *akcia*.

We had heard rumors about these early after the Nazis had invaded Poland and the reports had continued as they marched eastward. Timush warned us that they would come to Tluste as well. We decided it was time to build a hiding place in our apartment. By this time, Jews all over Nazi-occupied Europe were building and creating hiding places to escape these raids. But the Germans and their local sympathizers were getting ever more astute at discovering these.

Timush was very mechanically minded and offered to help us. Most of the Jews we knew were not very handy with designing and building skills. In fact, they hardly knew how to hold or use a shovel. Everyone in my family was just as inept at those skills. So, we gratefully and enthusiastically accepted Timush's offer. With his help, we decided upon a unique spot for the entrance. It was one we were certain the Nazis had never seen—in the kitchen floor right under the stove. We were confident that no one would suspect a hiding place under this heavy cast iron oven. The plan would require someone on the outside to push the stove back in place after everyone else was inside and to make sure there were hot coals smoldering away inside. That final touch would further deflect any suspicion that anything was below it. Timush offered to do this for us anytime an akcia occurred. Reassured of the shrewdness of the plan we began work immediately.

With his expert help we had it dug out within a few days. The hiding place would not be expansive and was only meant to conceal us for a few hours or perhaps a couple of days at most. It was little more than a narrow tunnel—impossible to stand up in, but wide enough to allow two rows of six or seven people. So we could squeeze twelve to fourteen people total in it at a time.

Sometime after that, Timush came to us with a warning of an akcia that was to take place very soon. We quickly fled to the kitchen and moved back the stove. Timush patiently waited as we all descended into the hollowed-out hiding place. He shoved the oven back into place to cover the entrance. It still burned hot with coals from the evening meal, further ensuring any Jew hunters that there was nothing out of place at this spot in the house. We waited quietly with fear and trepidation as the noise of the akcia grew and climaxed.

It seems impossible amid the terror of these experiences, but there were some moments in the horror of what we faced that I can only recount as humorous. Looking back, it's possible to laugh now, but at the time we knew the deadly seriousness of our position. On this occasion, our immediate family was hiding in the bunker, but we had also allowed some of our neighbors to come in with us. One of these neighbors was an obese man who brought a pot of beans with him. In response to our expressions of surprise, he said, "I don't know how long I am going to be in here. What if I get hungry?" No sooner than he had sat down, he began to eat them.

Another neighbor in our company at the time was an artist and a dancer who had come from Hungary. He was trim and fit and seemed very serious-minded. Not long after we had been sealed in, we were waiting quietly and listening intently for any clues to what was happening above us. The mood was tense and we were all gripped by fear. But the beans were starting to take effect on our fat friend.

Suddenly, with no warning, the silence was broken with rumblings as the man began to flatulate loudly. In any other circumstance, the noise would have evoked immediate laughter. But there was little to laugh at in our desperate situation—there was only stunned silence from the others of us confined to the bunker as the air filled with the putrid smell. At this point the Hungarian artist calmly approached the corpulent man and stared directly into his eyes for a few moments. "Thank you very much!" he jabbed with an indignant look on his face. Then he turned and sat back down with his face toward the floor.

With a surprised look, the offender retorted, "Why are you thanking me?" The artist looked up and without hesitation said with a touch of anger, "Thank you that you didn't shit!" There was no laughter from us then, but the scene was burned in my memory, and out of the darkness of that horrible moment, I can look back now and laugh at the quick wit of that man.

The akcia continued on that occasion, but fortunately it didn't last long. Such incidences could vary quite significantly—from major sweeps gathering hundreds of Jews, to small events targeting just a few unfortunate ones. Often members of the Gestapo from the nearby town of Czortkow, which had a Gestapo office, instigated them. Sometimes, it would only be a few officers looking for some excitement: they would fly into our village to grab one or two Jews, killing them on the spot—and then it would be over. Other times it was more orchestrated and systematic, with the intent to rid the targeted area completely of Jews, to make it *Judenrein*, or 'rid of Jews.' That night we were spared of the latter.

I can laugh at our obese neighbor's digestive problems now, but I had a similarly embarrassing moment during another akcia. Not long after the event I've just recounted, I was visiting a friend nearby whose family also had a bunker in their house. My friend's name was Wilo Schechner and his father was a member of the local Judenrat. His mother had died a few years before the war. While we were playing together, news came suddenly that Gestapo agents from Czortkow were coming once again.

We heard the commotion from another room in my friend's house. His father was nervously moving about making preparations to hide. We rushed to see what was the reason for all the noise. My friend's father looked at me and said, "Akcia! Akcia! Go now! Run home, run home!" And he waved at me as if to push me out the door. He was afraid to reveal the place of their bunker just like so many others who had them. The fewer people who knew about the hiding places, the better chance they could remain undiscovered. But my friend grabbed my arm and pulled me close to him. "No!" he cried out. "He must stay here. He will never make it. He's not going to leave. Where I am going, he is going!"

His father quickly relented and we descended into the bunker as fast as we could. We sealed it up and waited. For a long time, there was silence. But then we heard pounding and loud voices shouting. The ceiling above us rattled with the heavy footsteps. We could not see them of course, but we knew they were members of the *Sonderdienst*, a special force created to eliminate Jews all over Europe. They and their local Ukrainian accomplices trampled all through the house, desperately looking for Jews. Throughout the afternoon and well into the evening we heard them combing every inch of the house, ripping open doors and pulling back panels from the walls. We listened to the noise and shouting from the streets just outside the house.

After a while, the noise settled down, but we were not sure when it would be safe for us to come out. So, we sat, motionless and quiet through the rest of the night. Sometime in the early morning hours, I began to feel sick. My stomach was churning from the fear and terror of it all. Soon I was feeling the need to relieve myself. But the pressure wasn't normal. I soon realized I had diarrhea. I tried hard to hold it back but some was already seeping out. Suddenly I lost all control of my functions and I could no longer hold it in. All I could think was, "Oh my God! I have shit in my pants!" The air filled with a stench that was so intense the others there began to cough and gag. Nothing was said, but it was evident from the looks on their faces that they were ready to kill me.

This time for sure it was no laughing matter, especially for me. And besides being terribly embarrassed, I was terribly frightened. Here I had been 'invited' reluctantly into my friend's family's hiding place, and now I was adding to their despair through my incontinence.

A few hours later, in the middle of the next day, all the noise finally died down. We felt it was now safe to come out. As you can imagine my parents were terrified when I didn't return home during the akcia. After it was over, my mother and sister went searching through the streets of Tluste looking at all the dead, fearful that I might be among them. They kept their hopes up that I hadn't been killed and those hopes were bolstered when they didn't find me there.

When I finally got home and came through the door, screams of relief and tears of joy filled the house. They grabbed me and hugged me as if they would never let me go. We learned later that about 40 people had been killed during that akcia.

12   FINDING FOOD

Trying to get enough food to stay alive was a constant struggle, so we were always looking for ways to find any extra bit to eat no matter how tiny. Sometimes those attempts put us at terrible risk for punishment or death.

The Nazis were, in effect, starving us to death by keeping us confined to the ghetto and providing as little food as possible. As I noted earlier, we were forbidden to go to the shops in town and the only way to get food was to find creative ways to smuggle it in.

My father had been sent to work in a local granary, where the job required him to load and carry 50- and 100-pound sacks of flour and other grains. Father was a businessman and had never done hard manual work in his life, having spent most of his working life sitting behind a desk. Now in his mid 40's, he was suddenly being ordered to do this very tough physical work. On top of that, he was already weak from hunger, and the rations given us were nowhere enough to sustain him. We were very fearful he wouldn't last long. One day as my sister passed by the place he was working, she tried hard to see inside and look for him. It turned out he was there in full view, but he was so frail and weak and covered in dust and dirt, she couldn't recognize him.

It was a terrible time for him, but while working there, he thought of a way to bring us a bit more food. One day before he dressed for work, he cut out holes in the front pockets of his pants. He put the pair on, sat down with some string tied up the bottom of each leg of those trousers. After that, he took another pair of pants and again cut out holes in the bottom of the front pockets. Then he slipped these pants over the ones he had tied, and put on his shoes.

That evening when he returned from work, he asked my mother to get the large washbasin and bring it to him. She got it and handed it to him. He sat it down on the floor and took off the top pair of pants. Then he stepped into the basin and reached down to untie the string on the cuffs. As the cords came off a shower of grain spilled out into the bucket. During the workday, Father had taken every chance to scoop up any bit of grain that dropped from the sacks and slip it through the holes in both pairs of pants. He often had to sweep the floors in the granary and that gave him even more opportunities to stealthily drop in a few kernels throughout the day.

It is amazing to think back now and remember how only a few ounces of flour could bring so much relief and joy to us. But it also brought fear and dread, because we knew our father was doing this at significant risk. Had he been caught, he would certainly have been shot then and there. These murderous rulers and their Ukrainian cohorts welcomed any excuse to eliminate another Jew, and the slightest offense was all they needed. Soon after this, in one of my attempts to get the family more food, I thought my time had come to be one of those excuses.

When food was in especially short supply and we felt desperate, we knew there might be scraps of food thrown out in the trash by others in the town. So, I would comb through every rubbish bin I came across. It was common to find scraps of vegetables that hadn't yet rotted and these bits and pieces helped keep us from starving.

One afternoon, my mother came to me and asked me to make one of these rounds. On this particular day, I had been lucky to find a few bits of vegetables and other scraps of food. Proud and happy with my success, I started for home. As I turned the last corner, I could see my house in view and there were only a few more steps to go. Suddenly I felt a hand come down swiftly and forcefully on my shoulder. My shirt pulled up around my neck and I couldn't move another step. I looked up to see one of the town's Ukrainian policemen, a man I knew by the name of Schap. He was known for being ill-tempered and violent towards the Jews. Like so many antisemites he derived a sadistic pleasure from his attacks on them.

He barked at me in threatening tones, "What are you doing here?" With a tremor in my voice, I shot back, "I'm going home!" His anger and hatred welled up as he raised his hand to strike me. His palm came down fast and furiously, smashing into my cheek. The pain was shocking. I had never been beaten or even hit before like this. Fear coursed through my veins and I tried to pull away, but it was no use—he had me firmly in his grip. What was he going to do to me? Would I be taken away from my family?

Suddenly I saw my mother running toward us. She cried out, "Come here Lonek! What are you doing outside?" Then she spoke to the policeman, "I will take him home, and I am going to punish him for going outside. He knows better. Can you please let him go?" His surprise in seeing her appear so abruptly disarmed him, and he relaxed his grip. He looked at my mother for a few seconds then completely released me. My mother wasted no time taking hold of me and dragging me toward our house. Another narrow escape for me, but this time the pain from having been struck made the fear all that much more intense. Little did I know that with each successive encounter with these killers, their brutality would ratchet up.

13 MY FRIEND RISKS HIS LIFE
FOR ME

A few weeks later I went to see my good friend Sam. I loved going to his house because his father had a workshop that for me was like a toyshop or a playground. Sam's father was a tinsmith and had so many tools of every shape and size—hammers, huge shears, workbenches with clamps and anvils affixed to them. And of course, many other interesting devices meant for various specific jobs. For today's kids, who have so many toys and electronics to play with, these instruments might inspire only boredom. But for a child in the early part of the 20th century, in a poorer part of the world, these were magical and to hold them and pretend to be building something was quite a treat.

When I met up with Sam that day, we went straight to the shop and began to let our imagination run wild. His father was there working on something as well. After playing for only a short time, we suddenly heard the Ukrainian police and the *Sonderdienst* scouring the town, banging on doors and shouting for Jews to come out. "Juden raus! Juden raus!" was the demand that echoed through the town. Sam's father jumped to the door and pulled down the wooden plank used to barricade the door. Sam and I quickly darted under a workbench and I pulled a cloth from off the table to cover me up. I lay perfectly still even though I was breathing very hard.

All at once there was a pounding on the door. It was one of the Ukrainian policemen, demanding that everyone inside was to come out immediately. Sam's father knew he would break the door open, so rather than let him come in he ran to it and pulled it open. The man raised his club and struck him knocking him to the ground. Then he reached down, grabbed Sam's father by the collar and pulled him outside, shoving him toward a group of Jews in the street who had already been captured. Then he returned to the doorway and shouted, "Anyone else in there? Come out now!" Often these assassins were afraid to come too quickly into the houses they were searching, for fear of someone hiding might ambush them. So, he stood still for a moment and cautiously began to move ahead through the doorway.

The bright sunlight from outside made it difficult for him to see the inside of the room clearly. He placed a hand over one of his eyes and bent his head forward to adjust his eyes to the dark. Stopping again, he repeated his demand, "Come out now!"

At that moment, Sam jumped up from behind the bench and ran at him screaming, "I'm here! I'm coming! There's no one else!" The policeman grabbed him by the shirt, struck him across his face and quickly exited dragging Sam to where the other Jews waited in the street. My heart leapt into my chest. What had Sam done? He had given himself up to them! And in the process, he had deflected the hunter's attention away from me. I listened carefully, fully expecting the soldier to return and turn over everything in the shop to expose me. Only a few minutes passed but they felt like hours. I heard no returning footsteps. I waited a little while longer, and it seemed increasingly likely that the soldier must have accepted Sam's claim that he was the only one left. Nevertheless, I continued to lie motionless on the floor under the bench, my heart pounding with fear.

By now the number of captives was growing in the street just outside the shop, and the Nazi soldiers ordered them to line up in rows of four. They were organizing them so they could march them to the outside of town to deport them to concentration and work camps. Sam joined their ranks toward the rear of the line and stood quietly waiting for his ordeal to begin. He looked around and noticed that the soldiers had moved toward the front and now couldn't see him since the others in the formation were adults and towered over him. He looked down the street—one so familiar to him that he knew every twist and turn and every passageway that branched off between the houses and shops that lined it. He saw one of those little alleys just a few yards in front of him and quickly assessed the distance and his chances of making it to it unnoticed. Could he dart toward it and slip into the narrow opening before one of the soldiers would notice or react? If he failed, it would almost certainly mean instant death. But if he stayed in the ranks, it could mean death as well. It might only mean delaying it by a few days or weeks or hours. The purpose of this particular akcia might be to acquire slave labor for the war effort. But Sam couldn't know that. It could be one designed to eliminate Jews.

Without further thought or hesitation, Sam ducked to the ground and scooted on all fours through the legs of the other prisoners. This was a brilliant move since the guards wouldn't have been able to see him, hidden as he was by the others. He knocked against the legs of his neighbors and some of them couldn't contain their surprise. Some of the Ukrainian policemen noticed the commotion and sprang toward the roiling in the lines, but by now Sam had reached the alleyway. He turned quickly into it, and then rose fully upright and sprinted toward the end of it. The alley wasn't a long one and was blocked by an eight-foot wall. But Sam didn't slow down as he approached it. Already the Ukrainians were entering the passageway and shouting for him to stop. Suddenly with one swift movement and no loss of speed, Sam leapt into the air at the fence. The adrenaline pumping through his veins and nerves shot him upward with superhuman strength. His right foot hit halfway up the wooden planks that blocked him. His hands grabbed at the top of the boards and then pulled him over it as smoothly, it seemed, as an Olympic high jumper. He landed on the opposite side with a thud and rolled over on his shoulder and onto his back. Ignoring everything but the present need, he sprang up and continued running as fast as he could across the street behind the fence and through another passageway that led to the edge of town.

The soldiers turned the corner in the alley and stopped suddenly as they encountered the wall. Where had he gone? Surely that little boy couldn't have jumped this wall. Yet he was nowhere to be found. They looked around for boxes, cans or anything else that could have concealed him. But he wasn't there. Meanwhile, Sam continued running toward a nearby stable and he darted toward it. He ran inside and ducked under the door of one of the stalls. It was empty but had a big mound of hay. He covered himself completely and tried to calm his heavy breathing and pounding heart. After a while he could tell it was quiet and no one had discovered his escape route. But he did not come out too soon and lay there all through the night and into the early morning hours as still as he could.

Sam had outwitted the Nazi soldiers and the armed policemen. He had once again employed the practical intelligence and street smarts that I had admired so much in him. But more than that, he had risked his life for me—a friend he had only known for a few months. He had been aware of what he was doing when he revealed himself and ran toward the policeman in the shop. In all likelihood, he realized, he was giving up his life.

We all knew by this time that when there was an akcia, to flee rather than be captured could mean death. There was little hope for surviving if caught running away. Had they found me, I wouldn't have known what to do. I wouldn't have known how to run or where to run. I didn't know the streets like Sam and I would have been too afraid. It wasn't lost on me that Sam had performed an amazing act of bravery and self-sacrifice. I had never witnessed anything like it, especially from such a young person. I would be and have been, forever indebted to him.

Back in the shop, I was unaware of the events that had just transpired. I lay still and quiet for many long hours. I am not sure how long but it seemed like an eternity. The noise of the akcia had died down within a couple of hours, but I was too afraid to come out, so I stayed there well into the evening.

Once again, my parents were deeply afraid that I had been captured and perhaps killed or taken to a camp. After dark, my mother covered herself with a shawl and crept out of the house to look for me. She knew I had gone to visit Sam, so she made her way there. It was still very dangerous and the streets were silent and empty as many people were still hiding. Luckily, she got to the workshop without being discovered. She entered and quietly called my name. I recognized her voice and crawled out from under the workbench and we hugged. But we wasted no time with too much sentiment and quickly made our way back to our house careful not to raise attention.

The next day I looked for Sam and I was delighted to find him. He told me about his narrow escape and that his father also found a way to get away. Once outside the workshop and in the custody of the Ukrainian policeman, his father quickly produced a gold watch and offered it to the policeman in exchange for letting him go. The policeman looked at the watch for a few seconds, then grabbed it from him. He pulled out his gun and pointed it in the air. Then he pulled the trigger and the blast reverberated across the town. He stared at Sam's father and then said, "Run now. Get out of here!"

Later on, in October of 1942, we learned that another akcia was being planned. My sister's boyfriend, Mendel, convinced us that we could escape by going to a nearby town where he had some friends that would take us in. My parents thought it was a good idea, but they decided to stay in Tluste because Timush had told them he would protect them. They were in favor of us getting as far away as possible, so Tusia, Mendel, Edek and I hurriedly left town. My mother and father stayed as planned.

Timush came later that night to get my parents. He planned to take them to a church where he had been working to replace some windows and affect other repairs. But as it happened, he couldn't go that evening, so he decided to take them to his own house for the night before taking them to the church in the morning. When morning broke, Timush came awake to noises outside. He rushed to the front door and opened it. The Germans were already swarming the area looking for Jews, and it was too late to take my parents to the church to hide them. He turned quickly and awakened my mother and father. He led them into his bedroom and told them to get onto his bed. There, he covered them with blankets and pillows and some coats, carefully arranging everything to look like there was nothing more there than linens and piles of clothing. He instructed them to lie as still as possible and not make a sound.

Hoping he had thought of everything, Timush then left the bedroom and slowly went to the door, which he had left, standing open. He casually leaned up against the doorframe and pulled a cigarette from his pocket. Very calmly, he put it in his mouth and struck a match. As he dragged on the cigarette, he stared out across the road like he was only a spectator gawking at all the excitement. He waited there as soldiers passed by and looked at him curiously. The locals assisting the Germans knew Timush was a Ukrainian Nationalist, and they convinced the soldiers to move along, since they couldn't believe he would be hiding any Jews. To further promote the ruse, Timush smiled at them and slowly turned—

walking out of sight into the house, leaving the front door wide open. For the moment, at least, this move alleviated any suspicion that might have remained about Timush. As the mobs passed, they saw the open door of his house and assumed it had already been searched. Without pause, they moved on and looked for other houses to raid.

14   TUSIA BECOMES A GENTILE

A month later, my father conceived of an idea to get my sister out of Tluste and to safety. He thought it would be possible for her to disguise herself as a Gentile. For a Jewish woman this ruse was possible, but for a Jewish boy or man, it could never succeed because of our custom of circumcision. If captured or interrogated, a drop of the trousers would reveal the truth of his ethnicity. My father knew it would be dangerous to try such a ploy, but he also worried if she stayed it would only be a matter of time before she would be killed. He felt the odds were better for her to survive this way and, as much as he didn't want to part with her, he was convinced it was better for at least one of our family to stay alive to be a witness of the terrible crimes committed there. And perhaps if she was successful, there might be a way for her to help the rest of the family.

He discussed the idea with Timush, and our Ukrainian friend told my father he would help. Timush had some close friends living in Krakow that he could contact to see if they would take her in. They decided that Timush would travel with her to Krakow under the guise that they were married. For the trip she could use Timush's wife's travel papers and identification. Once in Krakow, his friends could help her get other more permanent papers under her new identity.

At first, Tusia wasn't very eager to take a chance on this new plan. It was very dangerous and she didn't want to be separated from the rest of us. But finally, she bravely agreed to go, spurred on primarily by the thought that she might be able to help the rest of our family.

Our mother worked hard to find fresh, clean clothing for her so she wouldn't look like a destitute Jew from the ghetto. Tusia dyed her hair blonde, and studied under Timush to learn some Christian practices—including verses from the New Testament and some of the common prayers. When the day came for them to leave, my mother dressed her up, helped her apply some basic makeup, and fixed her hair very nicely. With her new clothes and hair color, she truly looked like an average Polish girl. Timush arrived as promised to take her away. My sister hugged every one of us with tears in her eyes. My mother and father wept bitterly as my brother and I stood by, laden with sadness. We had no idea whether we'd ever see her again, and after the other terrors we had experienced, we were not hopeful that we would.

Timush arranged for the travel to Krakow, knowing that they couldn't depart from the Tluste train station, since so many people there would have recognized both of them. Instead, they walked over 20 kilometers to the town of Zalishchyky where they could board the train without being identified. The grueling walk wasn't easy, since the cold of winter was already bearing down on them. It was also dangerous for the two of them to be out on the road alone. As they walked, it was likely they passed German military vehicles and soldiers whose suspicions might have been aroused. The locals who inhabited the farms, towns and villages between Tluste and Zalishchyky could have also given them trouble. The thought of the many things that could have gone wrong on the journey no doubt kept my parents wide awake that long night.

Eventually, Tusia and Timush arrived at the train station without any problems, purchased their tickets and boarded the train. The first stop was in Stanisławów, which was the hometown of my paternal grandfather. Here they had to change trains for the next leg of the journey. As they moved along the tracks and through the station, they noticed two Polish detectives checking papers and asking questions of the passengers. Tusia saw that one of them began to watch her intently. A few minutes later, the two detectives approached her and Timush. They asked for the papers and Timush produced the marriage certificate. One of the detectives inspected the documents, while the other asked some routine questions. Where were they from? Where were they going? How long had they been married? Timush answered all the questions while Tusia looked on quietly. "We are going to Krakow for vacation and to visit some friends there." The detectives seemed suspicious but didn't press for any more information. They calmly handed back the documents and walked away.

Timush wasn't convinced that they were entirely out of trouble yet. He noticed that the detectives continued to observe them as they walked through the station. Timush leaned over carefully to Tusia and asked under his breath, "Do you have any pictures of your family with you?" Tusia replied, "Yes, I do." Timush then whispered back, "Go now to the toilet and get rid of them. I am sorry, but if they find them on you, they will know you are disguised." Tusia immediately found the washroom, went in and entered a stall. She shut the door behind her and opened her purse. Slowly she took out the photos and gazed at them longingly. The faces of her beloved family soon blurred in her vision as Tusia started to weep. Sadness overwhelmed her realizing she may never see her family again and now may never have any pictures to remind her of them. Against all her instincts she slowly grasped the photos and began to tear them into pieces. The shreds of paper fell into the toilet below along with her bitter tears. Her sadness turned to anger and despair as she grabbed the handle and flushed it hard.

Tusia rejoined Timush in the terminal and he pulled her close to comfort her. He was careful to shield her weeping from the detectives, who continued to observe them. They were supposed to be on vacation, and any show of sadness might belie their ruse. After a while, Tusia regained her composure and soon the detectives were distracted with interrogating other passengers. It seemed like hours, but within a few minutes, it was time to board the next train.

It was a great relief for my sister once she was on the train. She had escaped the suspicions of the two detectives and now could relax for a little while. The train sped off into the dusk and before long it was pitch black outside. When it was time for most to be asleep, the conductors turned off all the lights in the train. There was some comfort and solace in this darkness for them. Timush held Tusia close to him and they tried to get a few winks of sleep in spite of the angst and fear.

Suddenly, however, the relief that the darkness had brought was robbed from them. The unmistakable sounds of approaching Gestapo agents shattered the quiet. As the agents opened the doors to each compartment, they shone flashlights onto the passengers as if they were searching for a fugitive. They made their way to my sister's section of the car and burst inside. Tusia buried her face into Timush's breast and pretended to be fast asleep. One of the Gestapo men stepped up to her and shone the light directly into her eyes. Tusia calmly raised her head and sleepily half opened her eyes, mumbling something unintelligible before closing her eyes again and letting her head drop back onto Timush. The officer kept the light fixed on her for a few more seconds, then flicked it off and turned back to the door. In seconds he was gone and off to another car.

Tusia had been a marvelous actor, surprising even herself with her performance. Her heart still raced inside her chest as if it were going to explode. But she kept her head down and began to calm herself. Needless to say, there wasn't much sleep for either of them that night as they anticipated the possibility of the agents returning and checking again. The train rocked on through the night and made its way westward, but for the rest of the trip, the fugitives remained unnoticed and avoided suspicion.

It took a full two days to get to the next station, a little town called Zegocina, where they would have to change trains again. It was morning when they arrived. Zegocina was just about 50 kilometers from Krakow, and with most of the journey behind them now, their hope grew that they could make it safely the rest of the way. It was a small town, but Zegocina had a major rail junction serving the city of Krakow and points beyond. As a result, the station was a bustling place and the Germans had many security measures in place there to prevent any threatening or illegal activity.

Once off of the train and onto the platform, Timush and Tusia quickly looked around and assessed their new situation. It was clear that in order to get into the station and to their next train they would have to get through a security checkpoint. On both sides of the gate through which they had to pass were several Gestapo agents looking for anyone suspicious. They were alert for anything and everything, black marketers, spies, smugglers and—of course—fleeing Jews.

Just as Tusia looked toward the gate, one of the officers turned and looked straight back at her. A cold shiver raced up and down her spine. She turned to Timush and said, "We are caught! I can see it in his eyes. He knows I am Jewish!" Timush put his arm around her and pulled her close. "Stay calm," he said, "and try to smile and look happy." Tusia did her best to comply, but then she noticed that the officer who had spied her turned suddenly to one of the other agents and whispered something to him. They both turned and looked directly at Tusia. Her heart sank and she dropped her eyes toward the ground as if that would prevent what was to come.

They made their way toward the checkpoint and as they got closer, Tusia gained enough courage to look toward the gate again. Now there was a group of people beginning to cluster there as the officers stopped the flow of passengers. They were intensely questioning two women dressed in all black with veils over their faces as if in mourning. She couldn't make out what the soldiers were saying, but the words were short, forceful and angry. Clearly these two women were arousing suspicion and the officers seemed ready to arrest them.

All of a sudden, one of the women turned away from the gate and began to run back toward the train tracks. The officers both drew their guns and cried out loudly, "Stop! Stop now!" The woman didn't stop but instead quickened her pace and darted onto one of the tracks. At once a gunshot rang out and echoed across the platforms. The woman fell flat on her face across the tracks. The other woman began to scream uncontrollably and then she too bolted from the gate toward the motionless woman on the ground. This woman made it only a little way before a second shot blasted across the terminal. She fell immediately to the ground as the hundreds of passengers looked on in shock.

Now it was all Tusia could do to keep from erupting in panic. These women were Jews, who had hoped that their mourning veils would hide their ethnicity. But the Gestapo men were not fooled and had no mercy for them. What now for Tusia? Already she was convinced that they had recognized her as a Jew and would be just as unmerciful to her. Terror welled up inside her and an overwhelming feeling of doom gripped her. Had she known what was coming next, that feeling would have been even more excruciating.

There was no choice for the two of them now. The officers had already spotted them, so they were compelled to continue toward the checkpoint. Once there, one of the men ordered them to turn aside for questioning. The usual questions were asked: "Where are you from? Where are you going?" Unsatisfied with their answers, the officer left the post and took them to a nearby interrogation room where another officer waited. They began to interrogate Timush and Tusia in German. Although Tusia did know some German, she told them she didn't understand their questions. Timush also claimed ignorance of the language. At that point the officers switched to Polish and, after learning of Timush's descent, occasionally to Ukrainian. Tusia's Polish was perfect, but she spoke Ukrainian with an accent. It wasn't common, but Poles and Ukrainians did intermarry. So they held out hope that her speech wouldn't be evidence against them.

Timush and Tusia bravely kept up the ruse, telling the officers they were married and on their way to Krakow for a holiday. Timush once again presented the marriage certificate and identification papers, but none of the documents had photos of either of them, so the officers' suspicions were not allayed. One of the men grabbed Tusia's purse and started to rummage through it. He dumped everything out on a nearby table and spread the items around to scrutinize them. My sister was greatly relieved she had destroyed the family photos—otherwise, they surely would have been arrested

Nevertheless—still unsatisfied and seemingly perturbed—one of the officers took a wooden box, turned it over and ordered my sister to stand on top of it. Then he told her to undress. At first, she didn't comply, but he shouted viciously at her and pulled out his gun. Tusia slowly began to remove her clothing. She took off her dress and then her camisole and finally her slip. She was left there in only her bra and panties when suddenly Timush cried out angrily, "No! Stop this! You are not going to undress my wife!" The soldiers looked at him in disbelief. But the sincerity and anger that came out in his voice convinced the officers to forgo this tactic.

While Tusia stepped off of the pedestal and began to dress, one of the agents picked up the phone and called for another officer to join them. He put the phone back down and slowly drew his gun from its holster. He walked toward her and brandished it in her face viciously, shouting question after question relentlessly until a third officer arrived.

The third man had brought a tape measure. He ordered Tusia to sit in a chair nearby while he began to measure the size of her head, her nose, the length of her legs, the breadth of her forehead and almost every other part of her body. As he did so, he occasionally nodded and assured the other officers that the measurements proved her to be Jewish. "Yes, these are the exact measurements for a Jewess," he asserted in German. He watched Tusia carefully to see whether his comments elicited fear and whether they might force her to give herself away. She could understand what he was saying, but she pretended she didn't in order to keep masquerading as a Pole.

Fortunately for her, when she became fearful or scared, she didn't turn white like most people. Instead, her face would flush red. Now she was certainly terrified, but anger began to well up inside her, and she was determined to hide her fear. Tusia told herself that, since she was probably going to die anyway, she wouldn't give them the satisfaction of believing their interrogation techniques could force her into admitting she was Jewish.

The men intensified their questioning, but Tusia didn't break under the pressure. Now and then, the officers would remove to another room to confer amongst themselves. Then they would return and unleash another round of intense questioning. After one of their private discussions, one of the officers returned and once again pulled out his gun. He walked up to Tusia and placed the barrel against her temple. Then he exclaimed, "We are tired of you delaying this! You might as well admit you are Jewish because we are ready to pull the trigger!" But Tusia with every ounce of courage she could muster retorted, "I am his wife! I am not Jewish!"

Surprised but still not entirely convinced, the officer slowly put his gun back in its holster. Then he turned toward Timush and started to question him. Up until now, the interrogation had focused on Tusia and nothing had been directed at Timush. Except for his protest against them undressing her, he had remained quiet in a nearby corner. But the ordeal was not yet over. They couldn't break my sister so they thought perhaps they could scare Timush into giving the two of them away. They knew he was Ukrainian and not Jewish. Why would such a man risk his life to save a lowly Jew? They seemed confident they could break him.

The officers began to interrogate Timush just as intensely as they had Tusia. They shouted question after question at him, the same ones they had already been asking, in the hope he would slip up and contradict himself. Timush continued to insist with great conviction that he and Tusia were husband and wife. Finally, when it became apparent that their questions wouldn't get a confession from him, the agents tried another tactic. One of the officers picked up a billy club and began to smack it against his palm. He told Timush, "There are other ways to get you to admit that she is Jewish." He walked over to Timush and clubbed him over the head. Then another officer punched him in the gut. They began to strike and beat him, all the while demanding that he admit he was protecting a Jew. But Timush, now bleeding all over his face and in terrible pain from the blows, somehow found the determination to continue insisting Tusia was his wife and not Jewish.

My sister sat and watched in horror. She was terrified that Timush would soon be dead or that he would eventually break under the brutality, revealing their secret. But in spite of the savage beating, he never relented. On the contrary, the sincerity in his claim seemed to increase with every blow. And he wasn't afraid to lash back at his attackers. At one point he shouted at them, "How dare you beat me? I thought the Germans were brothers with the Ukrainians!"

Eventually, the officers realized he wasn't going to change his story and gave up on this violent tactic. Again, they left the room to talk privately and decide what to do next. When they returned, the dim light of early morning was beginning to creep into the room. The inquest had lasted all night long. Tusia was exhausted, and Timush was languishing in pain. The officers looked tired as well, but they hadn't yet finished their quest for a confession. One of the agents announced, "You say this is your wife, but we say she is a Jewess and that you are trying to help her escape. So, we are going to arrest her. But you will go back to your home and bring more documents with photos that prove she is your wife." Tusia's fear gripped her as she thought, "How long will this take? A week or maybe two? My God, I will not die today but in a week I most certainly will!" Perhaps it would be better to admit everything now and have the whole ordeal over more quickly.

But Timush wasn't ready to give in. He shouted back at them, "No! You are not going to arrest my wife and keep her in prison alone. If you arrest her you will have to arrest me!" One of the officers fired back, "No! We ARE going to arrest her and not you. Get out of here now!" But Timush answered quickly, "In that case, I will sit here on the steps outside the prison and wait for her to come out. You have a telephone and telegraph. You can use them to get the information about us." The strength at which he made this declaration disarmed the agents and they left again to confer.

When Tusia heard him say this she thought, "What is he doing?" The officers had given Timush an opening to get away without being arrested and shot along with her. They were clearly convinced that if Timush left and failed to return it would be proof enough that my sister was a Jew and not his wife. Tusia couldn't believe he was ready to give his life to save hers. She was now convinced more than ever that this man, once such a feared antisemite, had genuinely repented from his bigotry and hatred. He was making the ultimate sacrifice to atone for all the fear and violence he had inflicted on the Jews of Tluste.

A little while later the agents came back and shouted to both of them, "Raus! Raus!" The German word meaning, "Get out!" Tusia quickly collected her things scattered on the tabletop and the two of them dashed out of the interrogation room, returning to the railway station where they hoped to rest from the trauma of the long night. On the way, they noticed that a man was following them. The Gestapo agents had sent a railroad employee to tail them closely and listen to their conversations. Recognizing the man was a spy, Timush began to act the part of an angry husband to keep up the ruse. He spoke sternly to Tusia, making sure the spy could overhear him, "You foolish woman! You died your hair blonde so you could look like a German. But anyone can see that it isn't your natural color. They thought you were a Jewess trying to escape. You got us in a lot of trouble! When we get home, I will beat you good for that!" Afterward, they went to a café and sat down to order. When the food came, Tusia couldn't imagine eating any of it because she was so despondent from the long ordeal. But Timush insisted, even though she could barely get the food down. He wanted to convince their observer that everything was returning to normal for them.

Timush and Tusia were so disoriented by the hours-long experience of the interrogation that it took some time for them to gather their wits and figure out the next steps. Timush found a washroom and cleaned his wounds. He knew it would take a while to recover from the massive bruising that he had received. Because of the full day's delay, they had missed their train connection to Krakow, but fortunately, the very last leg of the trip was a short journey. It was almost at day's end when they finally reached Krakow and the apartment of Timush's friends.

Timush worked hard to secure forged documents for Tusia so she could assimilate into the Polish community, but it was a difficult and dangerous task and was taking much longer than expected. After several days without progress, Tusia grew more and more nervous. With each passing hour, she became increasingly paranoid and reclusive. She couldn't bear being out in public. She imagined that every eye that looked her way belonged to a Nazi spy ready to expose her. She was so sick with worry that she couldn't eat much, and she began to grow weak and frail.

One night as she sat in her bedroom at the Krakow apartment while Timush and his friends played cards in the kitchen, she suddenly realized the men had begun to talk in hushed tones. Alarmed by the thought that they must be talking about her and didn't want her to overhear them, she strained hard to listen to the words they spoke. She could just make them out. What she overheard sent more fear through her veins.

"You know you are endangering your life," one man said to Timush in a warning tone. "For whom? A Jewess, that's who! She will be the first one to put you in jail when the Soviets come." If his friends were trying to convince Timush to abandon this mission of mercy, it was most likely because they were getting very nervous about being involved in this scheme. What might happen to them if the plot was uncovered? It seemed now that the only allies Timush and Tusia had in Krakow were abandoning them. Would fear provoke these men to denounce her to the authorities? The dangerous uncertainty of the situation convinced Tusia that they should return to Tluste. These people wouldn't support them if events turned against them. Later that night she shared her concerns with Timush and he agreed it was best for them to make the journey back.

On the return trip, they would pass through the same train stations as on their initial journey to Krakow. That meant they might once again meet the Gestapo agents at Zegocina. The day came for them to depart from Krakow, and it would be a short trip to the station where they had experienced the terrifying interrogation. When the train pulled up to the platform at the terminal, they stepped off and looked toward the checkpoint. Sure enough, the same two officers that had put them through the grueling and violent examination were there. Timush and Tusia approached the gate slowly, with much trepidation. The agents were preoccupied with checking and questioning other passengers and didn't immediately notice them. But soon they were at the gateway and the two men looked up in surprise, gawking openly as they checked them through. "Oh, so you have returned!" they exclaimed. "We are glad to see you. How was your vacation?" The pleasantness with which they greeted them caught Timush and Tusia by surprise. But they smiled and quietly replied, "It was very nice, thank you." The officers allowed them to pass without any resistance. It seems that their return convinced the officers that Timush and Tusia were indeed a married couple and my sister wasn't a fugitive.

Once past the checkpoint, they found a spot as far away from the officers as possible to begin their two-hour wait for the next train. But seeing these men again had filled them with fear. They decided it wasn't wise to give them an opportunity for further scrutiny by waiting for so long in the terminal. The thought of biding time with that threat looming over them seemed unbearable, especially to Tusia. So, they left the station and went into the village to find another way to get home.

From Zegocina they made their way southeast by foot, horse and buggy and every other way except by the train. Timush had friends in some of the little towns and villages along the way and arranged to stay with them. Most of these friends knew Timush but had never met his wife, so they didn't question Tusia's identity. One of these friends had been a prisoner with him in the Soviet prison at Berdachiv. Upon arriving at these homes to stay the night, Tusia would feign illness and retire to the bedroom so there was less chance of suspicions being aroused. More than once at these stops, as she lay awake trying to find enough peace of mind to doze off, she could hear the conversations. Their hosts were mostly devout Ukrainian Nationalists and, like Timush in his former life, they were rabid antisemites. Tusia listened as they talked to him about the evil of the Jews. Later she told us that she had never heard such slander and insult uttered about any living thing. The basest of animals—even a cockroach—couldn't be despised more than Timush's friends despised the Jews. Timush listened but didn't join in the derision. He sat quietly and didn't reveal his new way of thinking.

It was a tearful but happy reunion when Tusia and Timush finally arrived back in Tluste. We hadn't expected to see Tusia ever again, and even though we had hoped that she somehow would make it out and away from the horror we were facing, we were overjoyed to see her enter our home again. My mother and father broke down and cried. Then they sat down with Timush and Tusia and heard the whole dramatic story. The appreciation and indebtedness they felt toward Timush grew tremendously after hearing how he had risked his own life for their daughter. The friendship grew and we felt deeply grateful to him, but we had very little to return for his heroism. However, Timush never demanded anything. His vow to the priest was perhaps costing him much more than he had ever anticipated, but he never swayed from his commitment to undo the wrongs he had committed over the many years before the war.

15 TYPHUS

Conditions continued to deteriorate rapidly in the Tluste ghetto. People were starving and the basic necessities of life were becoming harder and harder to find. If getting food was difficult, the things needed for bathing, washing clothes and cleaning our homes was doubly so. As a result, it wasn't long before lice infested much of the community. This scourge was happening in every Jewish ghetto all over Poland, and a vast outbreak of typhus spread like wildfire through the entire country. So now, on top of all the other horrors, we were battling yet another threat to our lives.

One day my father became ill with an extremely high fever and had to be confined to bed. It didn't take long for us to determine he had contracted typhus. In the days that followed, he became engulfed with sadness and depression. The decision to stay in Poland rather than leaving before the war haunted him. Had he taken my aunt's offer to come to America, he could have saved his family. The guilt and emotional pain of that choice overwhelmed him. I am sure his mental anguish didn't help his fight to recover from the illness.

Father deteriorated rapidly after the fever set in and soon became delirious. In just a few days he slipped into a coma as his body temperature climbed to near-fatal highs. I remember seeing him lying motionless in his room, barely breathing with his mouth slightly open. Inside his lips, I could see that his tongue was black as charcoal from the fungus that often grows in the mouths of typhoid victims.

As a young boy, I didn't understand what caused this gruesome symptom. I remember thinking with horror, the fever has burned his tongue to a solid black. Seeing my father, who had been so strong throughout my life, lying there weak and helpless filled me with worry and fear. Why did he have to suffer such a terrible fate? What had he done to deserve this? Was he going to die? How could we survive without him? I don't remember how long he stayed alive after entering the coma, but it seemed it was no time at all before he succumbed to the awful disease. We wept uncontrollably as our grief overcame us.

During those times, arranging a proper burial was almost impossible. When a person died in the ghetto, the body was wrapped up, put on a wheelbarrow or some other cart and taken immediately to the Jewish graveyard just outside of town. The body would be buried as quickly as possible in a shallow grave with no coffin. But we couldn't bear the thought of such a crude ending for our dear father. We searched hard to find the materials to construct a simple wooden casket. We said our goodbyes to him. Then they wrapped his body in a sheet, placed him inside and nailed the box shut.

It was a very dreary day when the time came to bury him. It was cloudy and cold and snow lay everywhere all around. Four men who were responsible for burials at the Jewish graveyard came to carry the casket. They lifted the box and started toward the burial site. My mother and grandfather led the way with Edek, Tusia and

I following closely behind. My aunts Bela and Fryma also accompanied us. And my dear friend Sam walked with me.

The walk to the gravesite seemed interminable, but we finally reached the outskirts of town and the edge of the cemetery. The road that led into it was slightly higher than the graveyard, so we had to descend a small embankment to reach the grave. It was February and snow still covered the ground. When the pallbearers started to walk down into the cemetery from the edge of the road, the slippery snow and uneven ground caused them to stagger, and the weight of the coffin began to shift. Suddenly one of the men lost all traction and his feet slipped out from underneath him. He toppled backward and lost his grip on the box. The other men tried to hold on but it was impossible—the casket lurched to one side and fell hard to the ground. Its top burst wide open and my father's body rolled out onto the snow.

I looked down at my father's body and saw that the shroud covering him was soaked in blood. We all stood there gazing at the scene in horror. Traumatized, we cried out in despair. As the four men quickly gathered the body and placed it back into the coffin, we tried to console one another.

When the men had found a spot suitable for the grave, they dug it out as quickly as they could. In the meantime, we calmed ourselves and came to the graveside to pay our last respects. We were all crying, including my grandfather, who struggled through his tears to recite some traditional Jewish prayers. Once he finished, the four men shoveled the dirt back in until the hole was filled again. We watched, quietly sobbing for our dear father until the last shovel of dirt fell on the grave. A heavy sadness descended on me as I suddenly realized that none of us had brought anything to mark the grave or to leave for a headstone. The thought of my father's burial site being nameless and its occupant unknown consumed me on the long walk back to our home.

All night I continued to think about that horrible day. I couldn't relinquish the terrible vision of my father's body spilling out onto the cold and snowy ground and the contrast of the dark red blood against the bright white snow. I thought about the crudeness of the makeshift coffin and how it seemed so inadequate for a man who had been so successful in life. And I remembered the unmarked grave and began to fear that in years to come all trace of it might disappear. It seemed to me that these murderers and monsters had taken everything from my father, not only in life but also now in his death.

The next day, I went to see my friend Sam and he talked to me and tried to console me. In the discussion, we decided to make sure my father's final resting place wouldn't go unidentified. We found some scrap pieces of wood and carved his name and dates deep into it. A few days later we made our way to the gravesite and planted it firmly into the ground. As one could imagine, a wooden headstone would not last forever. Sadly, when I was finally able to return to Tluste a few decades after the war, I couldn't find his grave.

16   TO THE WORK CAMPS

A few months after my father died, Mendel came to tell us that he could arrange for all of us to work in the nearby farm camps. These camps were growing a plant called *kok-saghyz* or the *Kazakh dandelion*, which was used to make synthetic rubber for the war effort. Even though the labor was hard in the camps, those who worked in them were, in many ways, better off than those trying to survive in the ghetto. Conditions for Jews in Tluste were horrendous since it had become so difficult to get the basic needs. At least in the camps a little food was provided, and it was better than the scraps we had to scrounge for in the town. There were also persistent rumors that the Nazis were preparing to exterminate the Jews in ghettos all over Poland and certainly the one in Tluste wouldn't escape the same fate. With labor desperately needed to keep the army supplied with rubber, the workers in these camps were less likely to be hunted down and killed—at least for the time being.

We all agreed that the farm camps would be the best place for us, so Mendel completed the arrangements for us to go. Our mother decided not to go with us, because she didn't want to leave our grandparents alone. The horrors we had faced had taken a heavy toll on them and they were becoming more and more feeble each day. There were also other Jews in town that needed special assistance, and our mother felt an obligation to help them—especially the young children who had become orphans. So, our efforts to persuade her to join us failed, as she insisted on staying in Tluste. Sensing the worry we felt for her, mother tried to put us at ease so that we wouldn't change our minds about going. She even promised that she would try to come to the camp as soon as she could.

My brother and I were taken to a nearby camp at a small village known as Lisowce and my sister and her boyfriend were taken to another camp near the village of Szypowce. The two camps were just a few miles apart. I was still very young, so I was given a job as a water boy. This involved leading a mule laden with water barrels down the rows of plants. When someone needed water, I ladled it into a cup and gave it to him or her. It wasn't a strenuous job, but I was on my feet in the hot sun, pulling on the mule for hours, and was exhausted when each long day was over.

Edek did a variety of jobs, but none of them were as difficult as the work he had been forced to do at Kamionki, where he almost died. Of my sister's various jobs, the one she remembered most vividly was milking the cows. All in all, the work was hard, but our bosses were not overly cruel to us since they wanted the farms to be as productive as possible.

We were certainly prisoners in these camps, but strangely enough they were not fenced in or enclosed with barbed wire. However, they were located outside of town in a sparsely populated area, where the local people who lived in the scattered houses were quite happy to report anyone trying to escape. In spite of this, we occasionally took advantage of the lack of physical barriers. A few times we got away undetected to visit Tusia at her camp. Tusia went to visit our mother and relatives in Tluste several times without being discovered. But it was very dangerous to attempt so we didn't try often.

17   TLUSTE BECOMES A BLOODBATH

We had been working in the camps for a couple of months when a rumor began circulating that a big akcia was about to occur in Tluste. It was clear now that the Germans were beginning to lose the war on the Eastern Front, and as a result, they began to increase their efforts to make the entire region *Judenrein*. We knew that any new akcia would likely be much more extensive and severe than the smaller ones that had occurred over the past few years. So, we became fearful for our mother and our relatives still residing in Tluste.

One night, Tusia snuck away from her camp to warn my mother about the anticipated raid. She wanted to convince her to come back to the farms, realizing she would be safer there. However, my mother refused because she didn't want to leave her parents alone to face the onslaught. Also, one of her cousins had just arrived to stay with her, accompanied by two young children who had been deported from another town a few days earlier. My mother felt an obligation to all of them and was still determined to stay. She told Tusia that one of the members of the local Judenrat had assured her that no akcia was imminent, and if one were planned, he would warn her in time to get away or hide. Worried, but realizing it would be futile to argue any longer, Tusia returned to the camp.

But some of the Judenrat did know that an akcia was being planned and would take place soon. However, they were uncertain of the exact date. The father of my friend, Wilo Schechner, revealed in an interview after the war, that some of them first heard of the event on May 23 of 1943. From there the news spread to a few Jewish families in the area. Most of them went to hide in the surrounding fields and forests on that day. But as the next day passed and nothing happened, they all returned to their homes.

A few days later, in the dark early-morning hours of May 27, the rumored akcia became a horrific reality. Survivors of this rampage later renamed the day *Black Thursday*. The *Sonderdienst*, accompanied by their Ukrainian henchmen, took to the streets in search of Jews to kill. Witnesses of this most violent strike on our little town said the perpetrators were mostly drunk from a long night at the pubs, and were still drinking heavily as they began their assault. They marched through the streets and alleyways of the ghetto and began to pound on the doors before breaking them in. Shots started to ring out all over the town. The angry shouts of the attackers mingled with the screams and cries of the Jewish victims. The tumult began slowly but escalated quickly into full anarchy. People were dragged from their beds, half-naked and shoeless. It didn't matter their age or condition. Young children, babies, old men and women—many of who were already on their deathbeds— were forced out and lined up to be marched to their execution. The murderous riot continued even after the night gave way to the dawn. The rising of the sun did nothing to deter the hatred of these beasts. In fact, with the ever-brighter light, the noise and chaos intensified and continued well into the early afternoon.

Suddenly, there came an unexpected lull in the violence. The silence was a brief relief for those still left hiding in the town. Perhaps the akcia was over. But their terror wasn't yet to be allayed.

Ominously, storm clouds began to billow up over the countryside and thunder rolled in the distance. An hour or two passed and then the ruckus started again. The butchers had only stopped to eat lunch. That anyone could think about eating after having committed such violence boggles the mind. Their consciences were so seared that any trace of human kindness or mercy had long been eradicated from their minds. The Germans among them were driven by their twisted vision of a master race and the glory of the Third Reich. The local Poles and Ukrainians were after any scrap of bounty—jewels, trinkets, even coats or shoes—left by or stolen from the Jews.

In the middle of the afternoon, the shooting began again and it became just as intense as before. The murderers went back through the town revisiting some houses they had already cleared. Armed with axes and rifles, they chopped through the doors and windows and fired indiscriminately into the mostly-vacant homes. Sometimes they tossed in hand grenades just to be sure to kill anyone who might be out of plain sight.

As the next few hours passed, the sky darkened and became almost black as the rainstorm grew closer. Suddenly heavy rain began to pour from the heavens in torrents. Thunder shook the buildings and the ground and lightning filled the skies. But the deluge didn't slow the butchers down. It was as if they had lost feeling and sensitivity to everything. The soaking wet, the ear-splitting booms and the blinding flashes didn't faze them at all. Dusk descended on the town and nightfall came, but the violent noise still didn't abate. Finally, a trumpet blasted from a distance. It was a signal to end the purge. Gradually the shooting died down and came to a reluctant stop. The thunderstorm was now in the far distance but it could still be heard rumbling softly like the quiet sobbing of those who had survived. Outside, hundreds of people lay dead in the streets. Local Ukrainians tasked with cleaning up the mayhem pulled carts piled high with bloody, mutilated and lifeless bodies.

In the long hours before the trumpet had finally sounded, well over 3,000 Jews had been slaughtered. Many had been shot on sight as they were pulled from their houses. But many more were marched into town and lined up, waiting to be taken to the cemetery for a mass execution. As they assembled the hundreds of victims in the town square, the Germans called out the biggest and strongest men among the prisoners. They ordered them to go to the cemetery and gave them shovels to begin to dig a huge pit. Once the men had finished the digging, the Germans lined them up and shot them. Then they pushed their bodies into the hole.

Back in the town square, the officers and policemen began to march the captives toward the graveyard. They took one hundred people at a time and forced them down the road. Once at the gravesite, they ordered them all to undress and place their clothes in the back of a nearby truck. Then a few at a time were sent out onto a wooden plank that spanned the pit. On one side sat a soldier behind a machine gun. As the victims stood over the mass grave, he opened fire on them and one by one each person fell into the hole below. Not everyone died immediately, and as the bodies piled up the heap of flesh writhed, and groans of death rose up from the pit. When the killing finally stopped, the pit was covered over with dirt, creating a massive mound in the middle of the cemetery.

The summer heat in Tluste was already intense for late May. As the next days passed and the temperature rose, gasses and liquids from the rotting bodies sweltered under the ground and pushed upward to the surface. An utterly unbearable stench enveloped the area. The pressure from the decaying corpses caused the mound to heave up and down ever so slightly, seeming even to make ghostly sounds as the putrefying mass alternately swelled and sank.

In the early evening, as the air cooled, an eerie mist rose up from the grave and spread across the entire cemetery. This grisly sight haunted the locals who passed by. After seeing it, some even said it was a sign that the God of the Jews was angry and would torment them for the evil that had occurred there.

Meanwhile, at the camps, we were too far away to hear the sound of the violence occurring in Tluste that terrible day. The shooting, the cries, the screams and the sound of the machine gun firing over and over again must have echoed across the countryside. We were completely unaware of the destruction happening there. Yet it wouldn't be long before the news of that terrible day reached us.

Tusia had gotten wind of it, and two days later—once she felt it was safe to do so—she slipped out of her camp and made her way into Tluste to find out what had happened. When she arrived, she went to our house but it was locked and boarded up by the Gestapo and she couldn't enter. There was no sign of any life there. Later, she found our grandfather. With him were my aunt and uncle, our cousin and the two young children. Somehow, they had survived. Tears started streaming down our grandfather's face as he told Tusia the awful news. Our mother, grandmother and our aunt Bela had been captured and were killed in the mass execution at the cemetery.

We learned later that my mother had gone into the bunker under the stove in the kitchen once the raid started. But because of the turmoil, Timush had been unable to get to the house with all the commotion and wasn't there to push the stove back over the opening.

As much as he wanted to come to my mother's aid on that terrible day, Timush had been helpless during this latest akcia. The killing at the massive grave lasted for hours. All along the sides of the roadway the local Ukrainians and Poles gathered to watch the procession of Jewish captives as they were marched to the cemetery to be executed. Most of them looked on with delight as if they were watching a holiday parade. Timush made his way to this horrific spectacle and joined the crowds aligning the route. He watched in horror as he saw our mother marching along with them. My mother looked up and saw him standing there. She raised her hand in desperation and cried out to him, "My children! Please save my children!"

Timush couldn't speak back for fear of retribution so he silently watched her pass on toward the cemetery.

18   THE PUSH FOR JUDENREIN

The Tluste violence in May of 1943 would only be the beginning of a fast and furious period of terror unleashed by the Nazis. Documents found after the war shed light on this period and the plan for Jews in Galicia, of which Tluste was a part. One in particular, submitted by the head of the SS in Galicia to the overall leader of the SS for Eastern Europe, shows an increased effort to 'evacuate' Jews as early as 1942. 'Evacuate' for many of these Jews meant being sent to death camps. These 'evacuations' were carried out by akcia like the one on that awful day in Tluste. As a result, many were not evacuated as the documents proclaim but were killed on the spot as people hid or resisted capture. But the end result would be the same. By this time, the Germans had the intent of executing rather than evacuating and making the entire region Judenrein.

The next day after the mass killing in Tluste, Timush came to visit my brother and me at the camp and bring us the terrible news of our mother. He took us aside and with deep regret in his voice he said, "I am sorry to tell you Edek and Lonek, but you are now orphans." Tears welled in his eyes as he told us he had been unable to get to the house to help them. Edek and I were devastated and frightened, but Timush kept us focused. He said to us, "Listen, there are rumors that the Germans are going to liquidate all the work camps very soon. I am working on a plan to get you out of here and hide you."

We had heard these rumors in the camp as well. The prisoners there were frightened, but didn't know what to do. Many talked about fleeing the camps, but in reality, there was nowhere to go. The locals around the camps would be sure to expose or even kill any Jews trying to run away. Some considered joining the Jewish partisans that hid out in the surrounding forests conducting guerrilla warfare against the Nazis. But that was also a likely death sentence since the Germans were doing everything in their power to root them out.

On this visit, Timush revealed his idea to save us. "Now we have to organize ourselves and carefully plan how to survive," he said, speaking intently. "I have rented a large, three-story house on the outskirts of town. It has a big cellar and an attic with a turret on one side. At the corner of the property is a big square stone about two by two meters in size and twelve inches thick." We listened attentively to the detailed description. Timush continued, "I think we can build a bunker at this house that wouldn't be easy for the Nazis to find." His words filled us with renewed hope. Then he told us that when the time was right, he would determine how to get us there undetected.

Why he decided to give us such a detailed description of the house at that moment we didn't know. But these details became essential for us later when we had to find the home on our own. At that moment, of course, we assumed that Timush would come for us and take us there when it was time to go—and indeed, that was his plan. However, in these horrific and uncertain times, planning was often a useless endeavor.

A few more days passed and the rumors about extermination for the farm camps grew. We didn't know it at the time, but the effort to finally kill all the Jews left in Tluste was already underway.

Most of the rest of our family were murdered during this latest purge. Some local Ukrainians attacked my grandfather and brutally beat him, then hacked him to death with axes. We were never sure exactly how, but both uncles and our cousin, along with the two young children she was caring for, were all killed on the same day. On June 6, 1943, Tluste was officially declared Judenrein.

Now desperation was setting in at the camps among the prisoners. We had no way of hearing the news, but Himmler, the head of the SS, had just ordered the liquidation of all the ghettos in the East. Tluste was already wiped out and we concluded that it wouldn't be long before the order to exterminate the farm camps would come. Unbeknownst to us at the time, there had been an order issued to exterminate all the Jews in the local camps in the coming days.

As the rumors of terror grew, we nervously waited for Timush to come and help us escape. Several more days passed, but we didn't hear anything from him. Then one day, my sister and Mendel heard gunshots and explosions ringing out from another nearby camp. A few hours later, a naked man came running toward them from the surrounding fields. He was from the camp where the shooting had just occurred. He had pretended to be shot and then laid still on a pile of dead bodies to escape the assault. Once it was safe to do so, he ran away to my sister's camp to warn them they would be next. All the camps were to be liquidated on the same day but, in a bizarre mistake, the leader of his camp had carried out the order a day earlier than had been planned. It was tragic for the Jews there, but a turn of events that gave my sister and Mendel an early warning of what was to come.

Timush had promised to come and get them out of the camp, but was it now too late? In desperation they waited, anxiously wondering whether he knew about their impending doom. He must have also heard the rumors, however, because later that night Timush arrived on a motorcycle with a sidecar. Tusia and Mendel jumped on and they sped away from the camp undetected.

As soon as they were on their way, Tusia asked, "What about my brothers? We have to get them too!" But Timush said, "Not now. I can only take two of you, otherwise the neighbors near me will be suspicious. I will go get them in a day or two when it is safer." Like the rest of us, Timush was unaware that waiting even one more day would have been too late.

Edek and I weren't aware of that fact either. But like Tusia and Mendel, we had also heard the shooting at the other camp, even though we were a little farther away. We grew fearful that our time would come soon and felt a great sense of impending doom. Thinking the time had come for our escape, we anxiously waited all that day and into the evening for Timush to come. But there was not a word from or a sign of him.

Meanwhile, Timush, Tusia and Mendel were making their way back to his house under the cover of night. They traveled the back roads, cut across fields and rode on footpaths through the woods to avoid being seen by the locals. While on one of these forest paths they emerged suddenly from the trees to see a broad meadow in front of them where a group of teenage boys were grazing some horses. Timush pulled the motorcycle to a quick stop and shut down the engine. But it was too late. The boys had spotted them and were gazing at them with suspicion. Timush told my sister and Mendel to move back into the woods and hide. Then he grabbed a thick fallen limb from the ground. He dismounted the bike and slowly started toward the boys. As he approached them, they began shouting and quickly surrounded him.

Timush didn't say a word but raised the branch and slapped it against his other hand to signal he was ready for a fight. One of the boys lunged at him and tried to grab hold of his arms. Timush jumped aside, raised the stick behind his head and struck the boy to the ground. The others surrounded Timush and came at him in unison. He started swinging the branch in every direction, twisting and turning to defend himself on every side. He knocked them back one after the other and beat them off. Even though there were more of them, they couldn't match his strength and speed.

Suddenly one of the boys picked up a large stone and threw it hard at Timush. The rock smashed into his nose, breaking the bone and splitting open a gash across the bridge. Blood began to pour from his nostril and stream from his face. But Timush didn't cry out in pain. Instead he lurched toward them one last time and of one accord, they ran away. Timush started to chase angrily after them, but after only a few steps he pulled up, shook the stick at them and turned back toward the forest. He rejoined my sister and Mendel and they rode off toward his house.

The group soon came to a river and Timush dropped to his knees and began to clean the blood from his face. Tusia ripped some cloth from her blouse and made a bandage to put on the cut and stop the bleeding. Soon they continued their journey again. It was almost morning when they crossed one of the main roads and looked off in the distance to see an ominous sight. A convoy of trucks and soldiers was moving along the road toward our camp.

Tusia was overwhelmed with worry for my brother and me. Is it too late for them to escape now, she wondered. Would they know why the convoy was coming and understand they must get away? There was nothing they could do but hope and try to get to Timush's house as fast as they could.

Early that same morning, we heard the convoy of trucks rumbling down the road toward our camp. Had Tusia known, she would have been greatly relieved that we deduced it could only mean one thing. Edek and I put together all the clues—the weeks of rumors about liquidation, the shooting the day before and now the noise of troops on the move toward our camp. They added up to one certainty: the liquidation of our camp was about to happen. We decided it was time to act. We could no longer wait for Timush because soon there would be no reason left for him to come.

Quickly we assessed our surroundings to determine where we could we go and how we could escape. The landscape around the camp was familiar to us from the times we had slipped away to see our sister. To one side a meadow spread out and then disappeared down a small incline. It was a ravine formed by a narrow stream that flowed across the gentle plain. On the other side of it was a field of wheat. It was mid-June so the wheat was tall and hearty. If we could get across the meadow and into the gully unnoticed, we could make it into the wheat without much problem. There we could hide until dark when it would be safer to make the trek to Timush's house.

The trucks lumbered on in the distance but their sound was growing ever closer. We knew there was no time to waste now. It was still early morning and not many people were moving around the camp. There would be no better time to make our move. We casually made our way to the edge of the farm so as not to attract attention.

Once there, we stopped and looked to see if we had been spotted. Reassured that no one had noticed us, Edek said softly, "Run now." We darted across the meadow and stumbled down the hill toward the stream. We hit the water without breaking stride and splashed into the middle of the current. The creek was narrow yet deeper than we had thought. The water rose up to our armpits making our steps slow and awkward, but we pushed through it quickly and splashed onto the other side. We scampered up the hill and ducked under the wheat stalks. Stopping suddenly, we lay quietly on our stomachs and tried to catch our breath. Once our hearts and panting slowed enough to hear again, we listened intently to determine whether we had been seen running away. There was no shouting from the guards or barking of dogs coming to track us. For now, we were safe.

Carefully sitting up, we peered over the feathery grains to view what was happening at the camp. Within minutes the trucks were at the farm. Armed SS troops jumped out of them and surrounded the facility. The soldiers shouted for everyone to come out of the barracks and line up in the yard. As the workers came out, they realized what was happening and panic set in. Some of them tried to run. But suddenly gunshots started to ring out and we saw people falling all around. Others were rounded up and shoved into the trucks. Every few minutes, explosions punctuated the chaos as the Nazis threw hand grenades into the barracks where Jews tried to hide. Cries and screams wafted over the top of the furious noise. It was a frightening sight and sound, like nothing we had ever experienced.

Edek and I waited motionless for the chaos to end. We heard the weeping of those captured and the groans of those who lay dying. Eventually the violence ended and we heard the trucks starting up to leave. Soon they were off and the noise of their engines faded into the distance. Once it was over, we moved carefully through the stalks toward the edge of the road. It was almost noon now and it would be much easier for someone at the camp to spot us moving across the field. We crawled slowly along for hours as the cool morning gave way to hot afternoon. Suddenly, we heard rustling in the wheat near us and then footsteps coming toward us. We stopped and lay as silent and as motionless as possible. We hoped we hadn't already been spotted. But it was too late. The blades of wheat above us parted and looking down on us was a big, burly man with a tool belt around his waist. He was a Ukrainian that lived nearby and he knew immediately we were Jews fleeing the camp.

He growled down at us, "Do you want to live or to die?" We didn't know if we should respond so we just stared back at him nervously. Then he barked, "Give me your shoes!" We were paralyzed with fear and so astonished we could neither move nor answer him. Then he repeated, "Give me your shoes!" His words finally sank in and we sat up quickly and began to untie our shoes. Without any more hesitation we pulled them off and handed them to him. He grabbed them greedily and looked them all over checking their condition. He tucked them under his arms and then shouted, "Now run! Get out of here!"

We jumped to our feet and raced further into the wheat. The sensation of running across the rough ground completely barefoot was new and startling but it didn't prevent me from moving as fast as I could to get as far away as possible. We made it to the edge of the wheat field and fell to the ground exhausted and out of breath.

The steamy summer heat rose up all around us in the wheat field. The balmy day was intensified by the rich moist soil that held the stalks and the heat caused the sweat to pour down my back. The stifling warmth was becoming unbearable but we knew we couldn't move for fear of giving ourselves away. I took in a deep breath, held it tightly for a few seconds and breathed out again with a sigh. We lay still in the tall stalks and waited for nightfall when it would be safe to move again.

Timush, Tusia and Mendel arrived safely at his house well before the morning light broke. He quietly took them toward the house and inside. Then he ushered them up to the attic and into the turret and settled them in to hide. Timush's wife, Hania, brought them some pillows and blankets to make a pallet, then made them a meal of soup and bread. They tried to get some rest, but they were too anxious about the fate of my brother and me. They were not very hopeful we had escaped, since the raid on the camps had come so quickly. The odds of getting away alive were almost zero because of the ruthless and cruel nature of the evil murderers and their all-too-willing cohorts in the local village. Timush tried to comfort Tusia and Mendel saying, "It is too dangerous now to go for them and the neighbors will be suspicious if they see me bringing someone in the middle of the night. But first thing in the morning I will go and look for them. Perhaps it will not be too late."

When nightfall came, we once again took up our journey toward Timush's house. It was a bright moonlit night, so we had to stay away from the main roads. We moved across the farms and fields, and cut our way through the woods and forests. We went up and down ravines and ditches and waded through streams and rivers. We had an idea where his new house was but didn't know the exact location. But we knew it would be a long walk that would take most of the night.

In the early hours of the morning, we finally neared the area of Tluste where we thought his house would be. As we walked down the road, we saw a large house just ahead. We approached it slowly and tried to make out its features. Then suddenly we looked down and there in front of us was a square stone that looked like the one Timush had described to us. Hopeful that we may have found it, we moved closer to the house to get a better view. Our hearts jumped for joy as we looked up to see it was three-stories high and had a turret. How could this not be the house? Could there be more than one house in the area that could fit Timush's description? We felt good about our chances, but considering the consequences if somehow, we were wrong, we didn't want to rush forward too quickly.

We moved slowly and deliberately toward the front door, careful not to make a sound. We saw that the house was completely dark. Knocking on the door might awaken the neighbors and give us away, so we moved carefully around to the side of the house and peeked into the windows. If it was his house, we hoped to figure out where Timush slept. We found a window that seemed to look in on one of the bedrooms and gently tapped on the pane. We waited for a few minutes, but no one stirred, so we rapped again.

Suddenly we saw someone coming toward the window. The figure bent down and slowly pulled the window open. It was Timush! We could hardly contain our joy at finding him but he silenced us and whispered softly, "Shhhhh! Be very quiet. We must not wake the neighbors." He pointed off toward the back of the house and said, "There behind the house is a barn. Go there as quietly as you can and hide there until the morning. I cannot let you come in tonight or the neighbors might see us."

We wasted no time and headed off to find the shed. All at once the darkness was split by the sound of a dog barking from a nearby house. We quickened our pace and pushed through the shed door. We pulled it tightly but quietly behind us and ducked down. After a few minutes, the dog was silent once again and we breathed a sigh of relief.

We felt our way around in the barn assisted only by a few rays of moonlight passing through the rickety roof and walls. There was a hayloft, and after a short search for its ladder, we crawled up into it. Piling up some of the straw for a soft mattress, we covered ourselves with more hay to completely conceal ourselves.

I lay still and tried to clear my head of the visions of people being gunned down. But they persisted and played back over and over again. I couldn't help but reflect on our miraculous escape. We suspected, and later confirmed, that very few had escaped our camp. Once the SS surrounded the farm and started firing it was too late for anyone to run away. By then there was nowhere to go. By a stroke of luck, we had been at the right place at the right time —near the edge of the camp and in the early morning—when we had heard the trucks with the death squads coming. Our decision to run before they arrived was a gamble and could have gotten us killed. But it turned out to be our saving move. Had we delayed that decision by only a few minutes, we would have died. And the peasant in the wheat field who took our shoes—he could have taken them and still turned us into the authorities.

My body started to tremble as I processed the reality of how narrowly we had escaped death. I tried to calm myself but the shaking wouldn't stop. Soon I realized it was not only trauma from our harrowing day that caused the shivering. It were my clothes, wet from sweat and traipsing through streams, that chilled me to the bone as they dried in the cool night air. I pulled more of the hay on top of me and the warmth returned to my body. I started to relax, and for the first time in days, I felt safe. My raw and ravaged nerves began to calm and soon I was in a deep sleep.

That night was the best I had slept in weeks. I don't remember whether I dreamt or not, and if I did, whether the dreams were pleasant or nightmarish. Either way, there could have been no dream as horrifying as the reality of what we had just experienced. In the span of just a few days our entire world, which was already a topsy-turvy nightmare, had been turned irrevocably upside down. Our parents and relatives were all dead. Our home and everything we possessed had been taken from us. And we were still being hunted.

For one night in the hayloft, I felt safe and at peace. But what would the next day bring? The monsters would come again. They wouldn't stop searching until they found us. They would bust down the doors, rip through the houses and turn everything inside out to find every last Jew. They would bring their dogs to track us down in our hiding places; dogs thirsty for the scent of any Jewish life that might survive to tell the cruel and horrid story we had lived. Could we escape such vicious determination? Fortunately, we had a committed ally in Timush and he had a brilliant plan to help us.

We awoke to beams of sunlight streaking through the narrow gaps between the boards of the barn. All was quiet and peaceful. Chickens cackled in the barnyard and a rooster let out a short crow. Suddenly our noses caught the whiff of freshly baking bread. The door of the shed opened. We stayed still and quiet, not sure who was coming. Timush's wife, Hania, stepped across the threshold and called to the chickens. She scattered some feed out for them then turned toward the ladder. She climbed up and in her hand was a bucket. The smell of the fresh bread intensified as she plopped it down on edge of the loft. Still standing at the top of the ladder she reached down inside and pulled out several round, flat loaves. They glistened with creamy butter and steam was still rising off of them. We pulled ourselves out of the hay and lunged for them. We were so furiously hungry that we devoured them almost instantly. She reached back into the bucket and pulled out a carafe of hot coffee and poured it into two cups and handed them to us. We thanked her effusively and began to sip the soothing coffee.

That morning's homemade bread was one of the most memorable meals I have ever had. It was what's known as *flam pletzel*, one of the simplest breads to make. A flatbread consisting of only flour, water and a little vegetable oil, it isn't so flavorful to average taste buds. But at that moment for me, that bread was like ambrosia, food for the gods. Even today if I smell or taste bread that is anything like it, I flashback to that moment and I get flushed with good memories. It is an ironic trait of our human nature that in the midst of such terrifying times, the slightest bit of relief from that terror can be etched deeply into our minds and become an intensely pleasurable memory. I will never forget the kindness of these two people and all they risked and sacrificed to save my family.

That bread, to me, became a small token and symbol of the incredible sacrifice Timush and Hania made for my family and me.

19 INTO THE BUNKER

The next day was one of mixed emotions. There was the overwhelming fear of knowing we were not yet out of danger. But that was offset by the joy of being reunited with Tusia and Mendel, and the exhilaration we felt as we reflected on our narrow escape. We had defied all odds. Yet we also understood that time was of the essence. We couldn't afford to wait; we must quickly determine the next steps to ensure our survival.

Timush was already working to develop a plan. After we cleaned ourselves up and ate a little to regain our strength, he sat down with us and, with excitement lighting his face, began to reveal his idea to hide us. We had come to expect his natural exuberance whenever he was solving a problem or outlining a solution.

Of course, a great question arises when one considers the kindness and aid this man gave us, and the great risks he faced in order to save us. Why? What was his motivation? Was it purely as a result of his prison confession and his miraculous deliverance from death? Was he earnestly keeping his promise to his late friend, the priest? Was such an experience sufficient to change a heart mired in decades of hatred? There is no doubt that his prison experience must have played a role in his actions. He was an honorable man and his word meant something to him. His promises to others and to himself were binding, and once made, they were to be fulfilled at all cost.

But in my mind, I always suspected there was something else at play. I wondered what else could be drawing this man forward, driving him to face his own death in order to save us? Timush, it seemed to me, possessed a sense of adventure. He approached almost every task with cheerful vigor. He enjoyed facing obstacles and designing strategies to overcome them. He had never attended university and probably did not have the best primary education. But he possessed an abundance of natural intelligence and street smarts. And he had an insatiable hunger to learn. Perhaps it was the skills of the mechanic within him, but he seemed to thrive on the logistical challenges of helping us, and from the danger that surrounded doing so. Nothing else explained sufficiently to me the sheer energy and delight with which he came to our rescue. A man who was under the burden of keeping a promise in the face of death may very well have the character to push on and complete his obligation. But to do so with the same spirit as one ready to engage in a sporting match... this implied something more.

It was with this level of fervor that Timush laid out his plan to us. His movements were energetic, and he spoke faster than usual. His mouth and brow seemed to be straining to hold back a smile so as not to reveal his enthusiasm for the moment. And he bounced a bit in his chair as he sketched on a scrap of paper the blueprints for an ingenuously designed hiding place.

A most bold and audacious undertaking revealed itself with every mark of his pencil. He began by explaining that, for any hope of success at this stage, a hiding place would have to be completely undetectable. The Nazis were now fully determined to exterminate any and all Jews, and they were dedicating all the resources necessary for the task.

The local Poles and Ukrainians were all too willing to assist, knowing there would be plenty of bounty from the victims to divide amongst themselves. And the thought that they could finally be rid of the race of people they had hated for centuries, added fire to their murderous bellies. Searches and akcia would no doubt come more often and with more vitriol than ever before. The hiding places that had served Jews before this final push of extermination would no longer be effective. The Germans and the locals had seen them all and were now very efficient at finding them and rooting them out.

Timush, however, had an idea for a bunker he was almost certain couldn't be found. Building it wouldn't be easy, and it would take a lot of hard work and cunning to accomplish without being discovered. Timush's sketch showed a room with the dimensions labeled on it. It was six and a half feet high, six feet wide and seven feet long. He explained this would be our hiding place. The size of the room didn't shock us, but position of the room in the sketch did. The right side of the drawing showed his house. We clearly recognized every level of it. But the bunker wasn't directly under it. Instead it was below the floor level of the cellar, but off to one side.

In his crude drawing, there was a large stone repositioned from the base of the cellar wall as if it had been moved away. Arrows indicating movement confirmed this and he explained that this would be our entrance. Once we were inside, the stone would be replaced, plastered over and painted to match the cellar walls. The entrance would be completely sealed and we would literally be entombed.

So many questions filled our heads as we gazed on the blueprints. How could we breathe? What if we had to get out because of a bombing raid or other emergency? Would this not place us in just as great a risk as if we were out in the open?

Timush was well ahead of us. He pointed to the drawing where the chimney stood. His finger landed on the base of the chimney, which came down into the bunker on one side. He had been careful to draw the details of the chimney flues on the sketch and how they would be left open into the underground room. Through them, we'd have access to fresh air. The solution for the air supply was truly novel. The problem with any underground bunker is the opening needed to bring in outside air. The vent creates a vulnerable spot that could lead to discovery by those hunting for hiding Jews.

Not only would air pass through these ducts. Timush had cleverly calculated that food and water could be lowered into the bunker through these flues as well. He would find just the right size of canisters that would easily fit the shape of the flues and slide up and down without being obstructed. Of course, what goes down must come up. The same system could be used to pass out our waste. The access point would be the flu cleanouts in the attic.

We gasped in awe at the brilliant design of this bunker. But Timush had more to reveal. He had a clever solution for communication as well, so that we could pass word back and forth between the fugitives in the bunker and the caretakers above. A thin rope with a bell attached would hang through the flues. If Timush needed to contact us, he could give the rope a tug and the bell on our side would alert us. But once alerted, how could we tell each other what we needed to communicate? Speech traveling through the long shafts would be distorted and difficult to understand. And the neighbors or anyone passing by might overhear the conversations. Timush had thought of that too. Another small rope would be lowered with a fishhook on it. To this hook, we could attach messages and notes, communicating clearly but silently.

We looked again at the large stone that would serve as the entrance. The thought of being sealed behind it in a small space was very disconcerting. If there were a fire, or one of us was in a desperate emergency, or—even more likely—if a bomb landed on the house, how would we escape? Would we be buried alive? Timush showed us the drawing of the stone again. On the side of it that faced into the bunker, he had drawn two sturdy hooks. If it became critical for us to escape, we could latch onto these with a rope or a pole with another hook and with suitable force dislodge the stone and the plaster concealing it on the cellar side. This design element gave us some much-needed reassurance. Now we could feel somewhat in control of our situation. We knew that this power couldn't be abused. We'd have to be very disciplined and resist the urge to flee at every sound or sign of danger.

Timush continued to flesh out the drawing. We studied it very carefully and with trepidation. Here in this tiny space, the four of us would have the best protection we could hope for from these monsters that sought to kill us. However, this new home could also become our grave if events turned against us. We were family and we loved each other very much. How would that love be tested in such close quarters? How would we face the test of being imprisoned in such a tight space for who knew how long? Would the denial of sunlight, fresh air and open space drive us to insanity? We knew there was no alternative, but these questions loomed large regardless.

The sketch held our fascination. We focused first on the integrity of the structure. Two thick wooden beams would support the room across the top. Those beams would, in turn, be supported by posts that would double as the frame for the bunk beds where we would sleep. These beds covered half of the width of the room, being three feet across and stretching the full length from wall to wall. The four of us would have to double up on the two bunks. My sister and her boyfriend would take the top, while my brother and I would use the lower.

A portable lamp such as mechanics often used would provide light for the room. The long cord from the lamp would run up the flue, where it would be plugged into an outlet near the opening in the attic. The light would be suspended from its hook in the middle of the ceiling of the bunker.

On the opposite wall from the bunks, Timush had drawn a sketch of a small table upon which we could eat, write or find crude ways to entertain ourselves. In the corner near the chimney flues was a makeshift toilet. It was a large metal basin with a cover that had an opening cut into it where we could sit. This section of the bunker offered the barest of privacy for our bodily functions. But Timush had considered that and designed it to be separated off in an L-shaped extension from the rest of the room. At least this way we'd be out of sight while relieving ourselves even if the sounds and smells wouldn't be hidden. Being very close to the flues would help vent the stench from our waste, but of course, it would never be completely odorless in such a tight space. However, this would be a very minor discomfort considering what we had already faced fleeing from the Nazis.

When Timush had finished explaining his sketch of the hiding place, he looked at us and eagerly awaited our response. We could see he was very pleased with his creation, and we noticed that inevitable sense of enjoyment he took in helping us navigate our harrowing ordeal. Our reaction was mixed, of course. There was no doubt his plan was ingenious, but now we were overwhelmed by the thought of building it to completion without being detected. How could we manage to do it and how long would it take? Would there be enough time before the Nazis and their local cronies found us?

The reality was, we had no choice but to proceed. It was this plan or death, and there was no time to waste. We all agreed to go through with it. Mendel, who had miraculously managed to hold on to some money, pledged it to Timush to help pay for the materials and other things that were necessary to ensure success.

The next challenge for us to solve was how to accomplish the work without arousing the suspicion of the locals. Timush and Hania had a six-year-old boy, whose name was Lubko. Since young children often don't understand discretion, his presence there posed a great risk for all of us. One innocent comment from him to a visitor or a neighbor and we'd be exposed. For this reason, his parents made sure he didn't know about the plan to hide us. But with all the work that needed to be done, it would be impossible to conceal it from him for very long. Hania felt it was best for everyone if she found another place for him to stay while we worked on the bunker. She convinced her mother to care for the boy during the digging and construction.

In the days to come, my sister and Mendel would remain hidden in the attic and my brother and I in the loft of the barn. Although some distance separated the house from the neighbors, there were four extra people on the property, and any noise or evidence could have easily meant our undoing. During the day, we tried to stay out of sight as much as possible. During the night, we worked as silently and as quickly as possible, preparing the bunker.

To begin, Timush took us to the cellar where we worked to remove the large stone. It was located at the base of the wall, in the corner edge of the house. The stone was about 15 inches thick, and it was just wide enough for one person to pass through that spot in the wall. It was heavy, but we steadily chipped away at the mortar and, rocking it back and forth, were finally able to remove it. The earth behind the stone was packed tightly, but it was mostly clay and so it loosened relatively easily as we dug. It would be a long process. First, we carved a tunnel projecting straight along the level of the stone. Then we excavated downward, in keeping with the idea that the bunker should be located far below the cellar. Timush, my brother and I did most of the digging. Shovel after shovel of dirt evacuated the small hole, and my sister packed it all into potato sacks so it could be carried out. Occasionally we'd have to stop and take the bags up and out of the cellar. We knew that the existence of a growing pile of dirt anywhere that could be seen by the neighbors or passersby would be an announcement that Jews were being hidden nearby. So, we carefully and quietly carried the bags only in the dark of night down to a small stream near the house and dumped the dirt into it.

For weeks we dug as fast as we could, all the while carefully considering our limitations as we strove to remain undetected. It was a slow and laborious effort, but with every passing day we grew increasingly hopeful that the task could, in fact, be accomplished. Timush worked as hard as any of us, sharing a fervor and concern that transcended the deepest of friendships.

It became crystal clear to us that he was genuinely committed to his promise, a vow made before God and the priest, to undo the harm wrought by his past sins. This mission, however, had transformed into something bigger and deeper. His devotion to our parents, and now to us, had matured fully into a love as deep as that of a dear and close family member. Even his wife, Hania, helped in any way that she could, although she was limited by the demands of caring for their young son. Hania's brother was also aware of our plan and joined in to help. He was a skilled carpenter, and Timush enlisted him to construct the bunk beds, table and chairs.

Timush supervised the digging and construction of the bunker, injecting passionate pride into every detail. He observed closely as the digging proceeded to make sure the walls and ceiling were not compromised and that they had full structural support. He brought in wooden beams to prop up the walls in the places that seemed weakest, in order to reinforce them even more. He dug right alongside us whenever he didn't have to see to other details or attend to commitments in his normal daily routine. Once the room had been completely dug out to its full size, he brought in plaster and coated the walls completely. This would help seal out moisture and add to the strength of the structure. All the wood and materials needed for the furniture were brought in through the narrow hole, and Hania's brother put them together inside the bunker. With his many years of experience, he made very quick work of it.

Now we had only to tackle the last details; our final preparations before we went into hiding. Timush ascended to the attic to open the clean-out access in the chimney, providing access to the flues. The ropes were dropped down through them, supporting both the signal bell and our messaging system. We tested them all out. We practiced a plan for any instance in which the ropes might be discovered in the attic, giving us away. The signal would be three rings on the bell, at which sound we would rush to pull the ropes down into the bunker, hiding them out of sight. Timush comforted us by saying he could always replace them after the danger was over. After that, the electric light was dropped down through one of the shafts by its long cord and plugged into an outlet up in the attic. We turned it on and it lit up the bunker brightly.

Timush's dedication to the plan and to saving us became an obsession that bordered on religious zealotry. At the end of every day's work, he ceremoniously stood in the pit and admired the progress that had been made. He walked over every inch of the room, carefully observing the structure and studying what needed to be done next.

Then, once he had taken everything in, he would drop to his knees and begin to pray. He prayed for God to help our crew finish this difficult task. He asked for protection from the Nazis and those in the area still hunting for Jews. And he pleaded that all our activities would go unnoticed by his neighbors. Sometimes Timush would ask Tusia to join him in his prayers. She reluctantly but dutifully obliged him. No doubt she had already experienced this with him during their trip to Krakow in order to keep up their ruse in front of suspicious eyes. And he had taught her much about the prayers and practices of the Christian faith during that time.

Perhaps Timush's prayers had indeed been effective, because we finished the work without being discovered. It was hard to believe that over a month had passed since we had escaped from the camps and returned to Timush's house. But now the work was completed, and it was time for us to finally disappear into the bunker. That night we all gathered in Timush's kitchen to celebrate the completion of our massive task. Hania made a wonderful meal for us and we ate with more frivolity and joy than we had in years.

After the meal was finished, we all bathed thoroughly, washing all of our clothes. Once clean and dressed we said our goodbyes to our devoted friends. With tears flowing from us all, we hugged Timush, Hania and her brother. We thanked them with our deepest gratitude. Then we descended into the cellar, towards the passageway at the far corner.

One by one we knelt down and slipped through the hole, dropping down into the chamber. My brother reached up and clicked on the light. All around him we could see our cavern illuminated, complete with furniture, stocks and supplies. We had our first stores of food and water packed in with us. On the table sat a small carbide light, for times when we didn't want the full light of the lamp above. We had our cups, bowls and plates and a few bits of tableware—knives, forks and spoons. There were cloths for cleaning our hands and dishes, towels for drying, and alcohol as the primary disinfectant. On the bunks, the clean and soft bedding looked inviting and warm. We had brought a few things to entertain ourselves, at least for a short time: some books, a deck of playing cards, a set of dominoes and a few newspapers.

We pushed these things around to reposition them while we settled in and tried to get comfortable in the new space. Timush shouted down through the opening that he was ready and asked if we were too. We gave him the go-ahead, along with one last cry of thanks, and then listened to the stone scraping back into its original place. We waited as Timush stirred the mortar and plaster with his trowel and slapped it into the gaps around the stone and across the face on the other side. In a few minutes he was done, and we could hear his muffled voice saying something indiscernible to Hania and her brother. Then their footsteps moved away and up the stairs.

A deathly silence fell heavily on our ears. Weeks of imagining what that moment would be like couldn't have prepared us for its ultimate fulfilment. It was an eerie and frightening realization, hitting us like the weight of the entrance stone: we had just been sealed into a potential grave. Paradoxically, we also felt a level of freedom that had been denied us for more than three years. Suddenly, with that final swipe of plaster across the face of the outer wall, we felt transported to another world: a world that couldn't be touched or penetrated by the unparalleled hatred and murder we had witnessed for so long.

Now we were here in a warm and safe place, which, for all of its constraints and lack of comfort, stood in wonderful contrast to the cold and cruel place we had abandoned. Here and now, we were ready to wait as long as it would take for the horrors and insanity of the world above to resolve, and a new world to be fashioned in its place.

In just a few weeks, I would turn fifteen years old. It was hard for me to believe. In some ways, the four years that had passed since our lives were turned upside down seemed to have flown by. But in other ways, they had seemed like an eternity. The next few months in the bunker would pass excruciatingly slow since we were now cut off from the natural rhythms of day and night and very little news from the outside world.

20 KILLING TIME

How long would we have to wait for that resolution to be reached?
It was impossible for anyone to predict or even to give a reasonable
speculation. The war by this time was about to turn but none of us
could have foreseen that. From the beginning of 1942, the Nazis
had pushed deeper and deeper into the Soviet Union with the goal
of capturing key oil fields to bolster resources for their war effort
and to control key cities like Stalingrad in an attempt to force the
Russians into submission. Their relatively easy victories against the
poorer and much less disciplined armies of Stalin had given them a
level of confidence that would soon be their undoing. By the end of
the year, they would be overextended and, on their way, to being
overmatched by the sheer numbers of the Red Army.

Timush had worked hard to get us into our hiding place, but for
him that wasn't the end of the duty he felt toward us. He was
rigorous in his effort to keep us informed and encouraged in our
charnel-like vault. He continually showed his overwhelming
devotion to us by anticipating what we needed to fight the long
psychological battle ahead. His empathy for what we would face

mentally while isolated for months underground preceded the fulfilment of the reality for us.

Every few days, food and water came down and our waste went up. But also, down through the flues came newspapers so we could keep up with news of the war. He had provided us with a map of Europe upon which we could mark the constantly moving Eastern Front. This daily task broke the monotony and gave us hope and reason to press on through the agony of being confined so deep underground.

During this time Timush would reveal another side of himself that I hadn't seen before we went into the bunker. Perhaps Tusia had seen it when they were gone so long to Krakow or at other times when he had pressed his affection upon her. Every few days, down through the shafts letters from him would come. They were beautifully written notes of encouragement, clearly intended to keep our spirits bolstered. Even more surprising were the occasional poems he wrote. They expressed his love for us and reminded us there was still some beauty that remained in a world so darkened by war and violence. He often wrote about our parents, helping us to remember them and telling us how thankful he was for the things they had taught him. He praised them and assured us they were in heaven keeping watch over all of us. He told us they would be ready to receive us when it came our time to die.

Timush's continued concern and care for us often brought us to tears. We wept while reading his well-crafted words, realizing the risk he had taken and all he had sacrificed to keep us alive. It was as if his whole purpose in life could only be fulfilled if we survived.

Tusia must have especially been moved by this man's devotion to us. She knew that a lot of his motivation was born from his adoration of her. Tusia could never return it because she was in love with Mendel. But no doubt she was flattered by the favor and attention he gave her whenever he had been around our family. She knew that his infatuation with her worked to the family's benefit.

Even though she couldn't feel the same way toward him, she had to respond carefully and delicately when he made overtures. She didn't want to lead him on, but she also didn't want to hurt him. I have always marveled at how graciously and respectfully she managed to balance this precarious burden while never violating her moral principles. She showed wisdom and strength well beyond her years.

Now that we were in the bunker, Tusia must have felt great relief knowing she didn't have to worry as much about balancing her reactions to Timush. In her letters responding to him, she showered praise and thanks on him for all he had done for us. She was careful not to further mislead him into thinking her passions were turning away from Mendel toward him. She wanted him to know that we didn't take for granted anything that he did for us. He had done so much already, asking him to do more was almost unbearable. However, there was one more very challenging favor she desperately wanted to ask of him.

We were still hopeful that our Aunt Fryma was still alive. All of our other relatives had been killed. But we had never heard any news about her. We yearned to know what had happened to her and if, thus far, she had survived. Tusia wrote to Timush and entreated him to look for her. She begged him, if she were found, to bring her to the bunker.

Timush was more than happy to oblige, but his wife protested. She complained that there was already too much work required to keep four people alive in the bunker. With five people, the added burden would be extremely difficult for her. The extra food that would be necessary and the additional waste to dispose of would increase suspicion from the local people. Perhaps the most significant risk was the one Timush would be taking to find her and bring her there. In the face of this opposition, Timush felt it best to give in to his wife's concerns. We understood Hania's worries, but our desperation to find and save our aunt was too great to ignore, and she became ever more determined to find a way to convince her.

Despite Timush's valiant efforts to keep us optimistic, hours upon hours of idle time spent cramped into such a tiny space together soon began to take its toll on us. As much as we loved one another, such close quarters magnified the petty irritations that people often have with one another. We could become annoyed easily by the smallest quirks, sounds or twitches that in a more normal time and place would have gone completely unnoticed. Meaningless and trivial disagreements could quickly turn into a raging argument. I remember once humming a melody from a classical piece that I was certain was written by Tchaikovsky. I commented on it and my sister contradicted me very curtly and said, "No! That isn't Tchaikovsky. That's Schubert." I argued back confidently, "It IS Tchaikovsky! You don't know what you are talking about!" Soon we were biting back and forth at one another in the most disrespectful tones. After a while I grew tired of arguing with her and stopped responding. And just as fast as it had come, my anger was forgotten.

Mendel was much older than all of us, about twelve years older than Tusia. Before going into the bunker, my brother and I tolerated him but we didn't particularly like him. He used to tease me, but not in an affectionate way. His ribbing felt more like mocking to me, and it was irritating rather than endearing. He had a confrontational personality that put my brother and me at odds with him many times. If we said, 'black,' he would say 'white.' And now that we were in this small space with him all day and night, the irritation we felt with each other grew. In almost every discussion, Edek and I would take one view and Mendel would take the opposite. My poor sister was caught in the middle and tried her best to keep the peace. My brother and I would roll our eyes at one another whenever we became annoyed with him. We wanted to complain to each other about him but there was no way we could do it without him hearing us.

There were other situations as well that caused my brother and I to wish there was more privacy to vent, or to talk about things we didn't want our sister or Mendel to hear. By coincidence, I had brought to the bunker one of the few possessions I had held onto throughout all the terrible times. It was a book that taught Morse Code. After one of these exasperating incidents, the idea came to me that we could start communicating with each other by code. But there was a problem. How could we keep our tapping silent? Then the solution came to me in a flash. If we tapped the code with our fingers directly onto one another's hand, we could remain completely quiet and discuss whatever we liked while remaining unnoticed.

The discovery of this new and secret way to communicate was very therapeutic for me. It was a point of comfort and relief to be able to have a private conversation with Edek. We had shared so many experiences and narrow escapes, he had become more to me than my brother. He was now my best friend. From that point on I reacted much better to the emotional tensions that occasionally boiled over.

Life became routine rather quickly after we settled into the bunker. Since there was no natural light, we were not bound by the natural rhythms of the rising and setting sun. As a result, we decided that it would be best if we slept during daylight hours and stayed awake through the night, to lessen the chances for noise that could be heard by neighbors or unexpected visitors.

We had a mirror to use for shaving and grooming, but we discovered another use for it by accident. If we held it under the flue of the chimney, it reflected the sky above the house. Through it, we could tell if it was light or dark outside and at times discern the weather. I spent hours with the mirror in my hand gazing up through the shafts.

As I looked at the tiny circle of light, I thought about basic sensations that I no longer could enjoy, like the feel of a summer breeze against my skin or soft raindrops on my face. There is something in the human spirit that yearns for the simplest of pleasures when denied them, especially when there's no way to know when one might enjoy them again. I have a new appreciation for the rain, the sun and the clouds after being trapped underground for months.

The thought of those simple pleasures sparked memories of the wonderful life we had left behind in Tarnopol. We longed for the abundant good times we had enjoyed then. To pass the time, we told each other stories about those days, doing our best to remember every little detail. We talked often about the foods we used to eat, describing their tastes, smells and presentations as vividly as we could. Tusia recited recipes for cakes and pies and meals she had helped our mother prepare in the kitchen. We remembered the songs we used to sing and sang them in quiet tones. We always enjoyed harmonizing and our voices blended perfectly. The music gave us great relief from the tedium. We played dominoes and cards for hours on end. All of these things did not totally eliminate the boredom but, without them, we surely would have been much more miserable.

Edek began to write a history of our lives. He documented the happy times of our early childhood but the memories of the past few years of horror seemed to dominate the story. When he sat down to write, more often than not, his pen recorded those horrors. To balance out the terrible past we often tried to imagine what life would be like for us after the war. We envisioned traveling the world, going on long vacations once again, getting married and raising our children and grandchildren. Without this hope and optimism, we most certainly would have fallen deeper and deeper into despair.

21   FRYMA IS FOUND

Day after day, Tusia wrote letters to Hania, pleading for them to find and bring Aunt Fryma into the bunker. She assured her that we would do everything we could to minimize the work and risk. She promised to pay whatever she could after the war to make amends for her efforts. Tusia even promised her full possession of the property that our parents and grandparents had owned in Tluste. She tried to convince her of the spiritual benefits that would come her way for saving another human being. She appealed to her religious side, reminding her of the "reward in heaven" she was bound to receive.

Finally, after many letters and promises, Hania gave in and agreed to let Timush search for our aunt. We were all elated, showering her with our gratitude. Timush began his quest, while we waited to hear any news.

Several days passed without any word regarding Fryma's whereabouts. We had no idea whether she had survived or not, but we tried to stay optimistic. Then, one day, a message passed down through the flue with the joyful words: Fryma is found!

We were overcome with excitement and prepared to welcome her. Hania decided it would be best for Lubko to go live with her mother now that Fryma was coming to the bunker. They had been very careful not to let him know that we were hiding there and so far, they had kept it from him. But now that another person was joining us, she felt it would be more difficult to shield him.

Timush had located our aunt in a nearby work camp. The prisoners of this camp had survived extermination so far, in part because of the efforts of a German officer who was in charge of the camp. His name was Vati and he made a successful case that the work being done there was essential to the German war effort. While life at the camp was still very difficult and the work was hard, Vati did everything he could to keep the prisoners alive. He was much more humane in his treatment of the prisoners than Germans at other camps.

When Timush found Fryma, she was in very bad health. She wasn't much more than skin and bones and the trauma from what had happened to our family had wrecked her emotionally. Naturally, she was very suspicious and fearful when Timush showed up to the camp to secure her release. She didn't know whether to trust his claim that we were still alive. When he announced that he was going to take her to us, she hesitated. By now the life at the camp was familiar to her, and she knew that she was in relative safety compared to what she might face outside. After all that she had experienced, she could hardly bear the thought of risking the move to a hiding place where she would deal with a new set of dangers. On top of that, Timush was very secretive about where he was taking her and didn't reveal much information about the bunker. His caution was intended to protect us and maintain the secrecy of the location. Even with the most discretion and the best intentions, information could easily be spread, and it was impossible to know whether treacherous ears were nearby listening. But eventually, Timush was able to persuade her to leave the camp with him.

A couple of days later he returned to the camp on a bicycle. Timush told Fryma that he would walk the bike a few yards in front of her, while she would need to follow some distance behind on foot to give the appearance they were not traveling together. That way, they would avoid arousing the suspicion of passersby and townspeople. Then they carefully set out in the prescribed fashion toward the house. The walk took longer than normal because of this cautious approach, but soon they arrived safely.

Once inside, Timush, perhaps a bit giddy about helping us once again and anticipating our joy at her arrival, began to feel a little mischievous. He decided to play a prank on Fryma. I don't think he was trying to be cruel to her; rather, I assume he wanted to infuse the situation with some levity and perhaps prove to her how well we were hidden. There hadn't been much opportunity for laughter or entertainment in those dark days, but Timush knew that this would be a happy occasion for all of us, and a good opportunity to have some fun.

Bringing Fryma into the kitchen, he pulled out a huge pot, filled it with water and put it on the stove to boil. He moved about casually as he did so, whistling a tune and making small talk. Meanwhile, Fryma's nervousness began to mount. "Why was he doing this?" she asked herself. "Is he going to kill me right here and use this hot water to clean up the evidence?" Panic began to overwhelm Fryma and her veins pulsed with terror. Suddenly she could contain herself no longer and demanded to know where we were hidden. Timush smiled and said, "Look all over the house. If you can find them, you can join them."

Now Fryma's nerves were fraying fast. My god, she thought. What could he possibly mean by that? Perhaps they are dead and he has brought me here for the same fate. Timush could see that his prank was getting a little out of hand and that Fryma had become very frightened. So he calmed her, took her hand and said, "Come with me." He gently led her up the stairs to the attic and positioned her near the chimney and the opening in the flues. But he was still enjoying the suspense in revealing the reunion. He turned to our aunt and said with an impish grin, "Your family is inside there." Fryma looked at the tiny opening in the chimney stones and gasped. "How could they be in there?" she asked. "It's only a few inches wide." But Timush, enjoying his little joke, wasn't ready to explain everything just yet. "Yes, I know," he said, "But they are, and if you want to join them, you will have to go in there too!" He was almost laughing now. But for Fryma, it was still not funny. She was confused and dazed, desperate to find reassurance that we were all safe, and that she would be secure along with us.

Timush tried one more ploy to keep the gag going. "Well, if you don't believe me, call down to them through the hole and they will answer." Fryma felt strange and silly. How could there be people at the bottom of a chimney flue? Nevertheless, she did as Timush said. "Tusia!" she called. "Tusia! Are you there?"

Tusia leapt up suddenly from the floor, where she had been lying in wait for any news of our beloved aunt. With tears beginning to stream down her cheeks, she called back to Fryma, "Yes, Fryma! Yes! We're here and we're safe!"

Fryma was in shock. She could hardly speak as emotion overcame her, along with memories of all the trauma she had experienced over the past several years. As her voice began to crack and falter, she fought to push out words. But she needed to know. "How... how... do I get in there?" As she spoke, tears rushed down her face, drenching her stained and ragged blouse.

Now Timush took her in his arms and comforted her, leading her back down the stairs and all the way down to the cellar. He had chiseled away some of the plaster from around the stone entrance, allowing it to be easily removed. Pulling it away from the wall, he showed Fryma how we got into the bunker. Shock still consumed her. She was speechless as we emerged one by one, and as we hugged her, only the sound of her sobs came back to us.

Timush took us all upstairs and showed us the boiling water. "Now quickly, all of you take turns at bathing while you are out here. Then, we'll have a nice dinner together before you all go back into hiding again."

We wasted no time and began to wash. The warm, clean water felt so good, it was very difficult to stop when it came my time to let someone else wash. We had been in the bunker for so long without bathing, and our skin, hair and faces were grimy and covered in dirt. Timush, in offering us the comfort of a warm bath, displayed yet again the deep empathy he felt for us in the minutest details.

While we washed, Timush prepared dinner. After we were clean and had dressed again, we all sat down. The meal was very simple, but it ranked among the most delicious I can remember. Reunited and nourishing our bodies with hot food, we were all radiant with joy. We had been given a small respite from our confinement in the bunker and, most importantly, we had our aunt back with us. We felt safe, knowing that we would soon be back into our perfect hiding place. It was good to see Timush face to face again. He was almost giddy that night as he delighted in sharing our warm friendship. There is no doubt he truly loved conversing and interacting with us. It was as if he longed to be a part of our family. And in many ways, he had become just as close as any true blood relative.

Soon, it was time for us to return to the bunker. We thanked Timush immensely for his hospitality, and he hugged us all goodbye. There was a definite sadness that crept over him as he led us back down to the cellar, so we could enter into hiding. We crawled through the narrow passageway and dropped down into the crypt, after which Timush pushed the large stone back in place. Once again, we heard his trowel scraping and spreading the mortar back across the face of the stone. Then he painted once more over the patching, concealing any evidence of a passageway and placed the sacks of potatoes in front of it. Once again, we were sealed away from the horrors of that dark and turbulent world above.

22 SETTLING IN FOR THE LONG WINTER

We had been in the bunker for almost three months when Fryma joined us. Now that she was there, we had to make some adjustments. The bed that my brother and I slept in was already too small for the two of us. We had to squeeze in with my aunt, as everyone agreed that it was best for her to sleep in our bunk. The decision was a matter of practicality. To put my sister and Fryma into one bunk would have been the modest choice, but there wouldn't have been enough space for Mendel and Edek alongside me in one bunk. Even Mendel and Edek in one bunk would have been too cramped. And, of course, it wouldn't have been proper for Fryma to sleep in the same bunk with Mendel. So, by process of elimination, the decision was made. I slept against the wall, Edek was in the middle and Fryma on the outside. We had to coordinate every little move and turn throughout the night. Many nights it was hard to sleep because I was so pressed up against the wall.

Though Fryma was overjoyed to be reunited with us, she still lived under the inescapable shadow of the shock and trauma she had experienced. Once she had settled into the dank and cramped quarters, the reality of the past three years began to thrust itself violently into her mind. What kind of existence was this? How could people be driven to live like animals, like rabbits confined to a warren, fearful of the daylight and condemned to hide eternally from their would-be predators? What had the world come to? Unanswerable questions ricocheted through her head alongside relentless memories of savagery, mutilation and flowing blood.

One might think that the safety of this sanctuary would provide a cathartic release for my aunt, freeing her from the paralysis that gripped so many other survivors. But Fryma's pain and suffering didn't end with her rescue. Her voice was gone. She couldn't muster a single word to speak, much less a sigh or grunt. Days passed, and still she said nothing. When we tried to engage her, she acknowledged us with gaunt and sad eyes. She couldn't utter a sound.

The other four of us had grown accustomed to performing our bodily functions, within earshot and smelling range, upon the crude toilet Timush had designed for us. But for Fryma, this was just one more humiliation in the long string of dehumanizing experiences she had been forced to endure. Here she was, in the company of people she knew well and loved, exposing her most intimate duties of life shamelessly. Fryma couldn't bring herself to the task. So, for more than four days, she withheld everything. Maybe she was hoping that the war would end so that she could get out and relieve herself privately. Though certainly not logical, you can't blame her when you consider the fact that we had been living in a world devoid of logic for quite some time. The day did come of course, that she could hold herself back no longer; the relief she finally felt must have overcome the shame and confusion that accompanied it.

When people live so close to one another for as long as we did, strange dynamics emerge. There is no rhyme or reason to the emotions that can take hold of a person and drive them to lash out. My memory isn't good enough to identify most of the episodes that occurred there, nor do I usually remember the feelings that drove them. But imagine for yourself how difficult it can be to live closely with the ones you love in a big house, where you still have the ability to retreat to isolated places and gather your thoughts before you say or do something silly or strange. The emotions we felt were the same, but in such close quarters as we occupied, alongside the overwhelming danger and uncertainty that loomed large over our heads, sensitivities are amplified beyond belief.

I am almost grateful that I cannot remember the squabbles and abrasive interchanges that we had. They seem so petty compared to the true enemy we faced. Here we were, coming to blows with each other over trivial and prideful details, while on the outside our persecutors were desperate to find every last one of us and shoot us down. That is a shame that I still carry within me, after all those years.

In the world above our heads, however, there were people who knew we had survived—that we had gone into hiding to save ourselves—and they couldn't stand the thought. Not all of them were Nazis, German soldiers, or the local rabble that had hated us for generations. Some of them were Jews like us.

Some weeks into our disappearance, a man unexpectedly arrived at Timush's house. The man was one of the Jewish policemen in the Tluste ghetto. He knew that we had been Timush's friends and had received assistance from him in the past. He had somehow survived the elimination of Jews in the town but realized the Nazis would come again and his luck might not last. He was desperate to find a more secure way to escape them.

Under the cover of the low light of dawn, this man quietly knocked on Timush's door. Timush, surprised at being interrupted so early in the day, reluctantly opened the door. The man spoke nervously but quickly, as if he only had a few hours to find an escape. Timush remained calm as he listened to the man's questions. "I know you have always protected the Kleiners," he said. "We know that some of them have survived the akcia, as well as the camp liquidations. Do you know where they might be?"

Timush thought carefully, taking his time to respond. But his cool reception to the inquiry dispelled some suspicion from him. At last, he replied, "I cannot tell you where they are because I do not know."

The man's ire began to rise. "Look! I think you are hiding them here and if it is found out, this could be very difficult for you. But if you tell me where they are hiding, and allow me to join them, I will not tell anyone."

A subtle smile began to spread across Timush's face. He straightened up and looked the man squarely in the eye. "I will tell you something. Not only will I tell you something, I will do something for you."

Timush stepped back from the doorway and pulled the door open wide. With his free hand, he motioned the man into the house with a generous welcoming gesture. "Please come in. I have told you that I do not know where they are. But you obviously do not believe me. So, I will allow you to search the house and see for yourself. Look wherever you please. If you can find them, then you can join them!"

The man's countenance fell as he sensed Timush's confidence and sincerity. But his desperation drove him, and he couldn't resist the offer put to him. He slowly followed Timush through the open door. Timush retreated to the kitchen, where he had a pot of coffee boiling. He calmly poured a cup and sat down at the table, buttering a slice of bread to eat alongside it.

The policeman watched as Timush took his breakfast at the table. He joined him in the kitchen and began searching the floorboards, the walls and the ceiling in the hopes of uncovering some clue to our whereabouts. But he found nothing, and soon moved on to the other rooms of the house.

It is important to note that as a policeman, this man would have been well trained at uncovering hiding places of Jews. At times they were forced to collaborate with the Nazis and German officials in looking for Jews in hiding. This man knew every trick in the book, and he could recognize the slightest sign of a hiding place. His search intensified as the hours passed and morning gave way to afternoon. He became ever more determined to uncover the secret that Timush was concealing.

He ransacked room after room, pushing back furniture from the walls and throwing back rugs on the floor. He stamped hard on hollow sounding spaces on the floor and pounded on walls where they seemed to give in a bit. Up into the attic he stormed, banging on every plank that he could see. Then, he marched down into the cellar. Flicking on the light, he surveyed the room's entire circumference. This time, Timush followed him. As he descended the stairs, he could see the official's confused and disappointed face. The stone walls of the cellar looked impenetrable, and nothing looked out of place. The concrete floor was fully intact and looked as if it had been undisturbed for many years.

The man stepped toward the farthest wall and moved his hand along the stones that formed the basement walls. He traversed every inch of the cellar floor, bending down and straining his eyes for any sign of a crack or a hidden door. Fortunately, the sacks of potatoes that hid the entry stone to our bunker didn't arouse his suspicion. He moved past them without a second thought. At last, he stopped and turned toward Timush: "Well you told the truth," he said, admitting defeat. "They are not here."

Timush shrugged his shoulders at the man and raised his hands, palms facing upward, as if to say, "I told you so." Proud that his feat of engineering had withstood its first test, it was all he could do to repress the smile that was welling up inside him. He turned and led the man back upstairs to see him out.

After the official had left, Timush wrote to us to tell us what had happened. The story gave us great relief and hope that our hiding place would never be found. We hadn't felt so safe and secure in years.

23 TIMUSH'S LIFE AND DEATH DECISION

The risks that Timush had taken for us over the past few years went well above and beyond the reach of any normal person's sense of repentance. His dedication puzzled us, but in our desperation to survive, we had come to depend on him completely. He was our only lifeline for escaping the brutality of the murderous Nazi regime. We were immensely grateful for all that he had done, and for the spirit and attitude with which he did it; as I have noted before, he became like a close family member to us, and it was as if he felt the duty to sacrifice himself for our protection. His love stood on par with that of a mother for her child, or that of a brother toward his sister.

Though we never really understood completely why he took these risks, we knew that his curious mind had seen distinction and sophistication in our parents. Perhaps their conversations had filled him with a sense and vision of achieving something that transcended his provincial boundaries. But there was another possible factor involved. Although he never explicitly stated it, we had picked up on ever so subtle clues that Timush was infatuated with Tusia. Such a love can drive a man to act irrationally, putting everything he has on the line.

Yet it was clear to him by now that Tusia would never return that love. She was in love with Mendel, and would remain true to him. In light of this, Timush's motives appeared even more mysterious. Was he, in fact, driven to help us by a boy-like crush? Or was he compelled by his respect and love for our parents? Did the tragic sight of our mother marching to her execution, pleading with him to save her children, stir his heart? Or was he merely keeping his vow to the priest and to God in the face of his miraculous near-death experience?

The probable reality is that all of these reasons combined into a perfect storm within his psyche. When that storm mingled with his intense desire for adventure, the stage was set for his most noble act of heroism yet.

Not long after Timush had returned from the Soviet prison, he had joined a Ukrainian auxiliary force that assisted the Germans locally. At that time, all such recruits were used mostly for police work in the local area around Tluste. Timush knew that being in this service would give him special access to information about possible akcia and other plans by the Germans that might affect the Jews of the region. And he was right—his decision to join had proven extremely valuable in protecting us over the past couple of years. But that decision was soon to come back to haunt him.

I am not sure exactly how long we had been in the bunker, but many months had already passed when we received the frightening news that Timush would be forced to leave Tluste. The men who had been conscripted for this local service were going to be sent to the front lines of the war. Timush, like the others, had received this notice, and he was required to report within days.

He sent us a long letter explaining the dilemma that we all now faced. The war was going very badly for the Nazis, especially on the Russian front. Their once terrifyingly efficient troops had been weakened, and they were being driven back by the sheer numbers of the Red Army. Since their massive defeat at Stalingrad almost a year earlier, the Germans had lost ground to the Soviets, and they were desperate for more men to fight—or, at the very least, to become cannon fodder. Timush didn't yet know where he would be assigned, but he was well aware that at this point in the war, any station would likely be a death sentence.

On the other hand, if Timush ignored the order, perhaps his chance of survival would be greater. He could try to flee and join the Ukrainian Nationalists that were fighting like guerrillas in the forests. These resisters were known as the Banderowcy named after their infamous leader, Stepan Bandera. They were not only anti-Soviet but also antisemitic. The other option he suggested was joining us in the bunker. But Hania was adamantly opposed to this and told him she would leave if he chose to do that. So, the only choice that allowed us to stay secure in the bunker was for him to follow the order he was given. Otherwise the Germans would no doubt eventually search the house. Would the bunker go undetected in that scenario? And even if it didn't, who would be there to provide our food and other needs?

Timush concluded his letter by saying that, for one of the first times in his life, he didn't know what to do. The decision was overwhelming, fraught with uncertainty, and he felt that it was too great for him to make alone. He pleaded with us to advise him on what he should do.

We read the letter a second time in disbelief. We were shocked by the news, and our hearts were suffocated under the weight of the decisive power he had placed before us. In essence, Timush was placing his life in our hands. We would be more likely to survive if he obeyed the order and reported to duty. His wife Hania would remain at the house to take care of us, and she could keep the supply lines running to the bunker. Regardless of his fate on the battlefront, if Timush obeyed the summons, his property would remain protected against seizure, and it was likely that his house would never be searched. But we couldn't bring ourselves to make this decision for him. After all that he had risked and done for us, how could we now ask him for the ultimate sacrifice —his life?

With heavy hearts, we penned our letter in response. First of all, we thanked him profusely for everything he had done for us over the years. Surely, we would have all died long ago without his great sacrifices. We empathized with him over the conflict and angst that he was facing around this momentous decision. And we expressed our great sorrow and regret for this new development. But we wrote that we couldn't make the choice for him nor would we attempt to influence it. We encouraged him to do what he felt he needed to do and what he thought was best.

As the letter slowly ascended up the flue our hearts sank. Once more we would have to wait anxiously. What would Timush decide to do? What influence would Hania have on his decision? Perhaps she saw this as an opportunity to finally force us out of the bunker and rid herself of the worry of being caught hiding Jews. Our fate hung in the balance although no one could predict the consequences of his choice. We waited for several days with no word. We wanted desperately to talk to him, not to try and influence his decision but just to know what was going through his mind and how he was leaning.

Hania indeed had her opinion about what he should do. Unknown to any of us at the time, she had been carrying on an affair with another man. We had always sensed that their marriage was under a lot of strain. And if we noticed Timush's constant attention and affection for Tusia, how much more must she have perceived it? For all we knew, he had admitted to Hania his desire for our sister. If she suspected or knew of his affections, no doubt it factored into her opinion about what Timush should do. It was clear that she felt the best course of action was for him to follow the orders and report to the front.

When the letter came down to us and we read his final determination, we were overwhelmed with a rush of conflicting emotions. He wrote simply, "It is best for all of us if I go and follow the orders." With his words came first a rush of elation as we also knew this was best for us, at least in the short term. But sadness and grief quickly followed and mixed with the brief sense of relief we had felt. We feared for him and our hearts ached thinking of the horror and suffering he would face on the battlefield. And then upon those emotions rode a flood of gratefulness and awe for this most unlikely hero we had found.

The enormity of what he had just chosen to do began to sink in even greater than when we had considered it the few days before. Had he chosen to disobey the order and join forces with the Ukrainian Nationalists instead, his chances for survival would have been much greater. But that would have been certain death for us.

Now this man was really making the greatest sacrifice of all. And no matter how much his decision was made with him and his family as his primary consideration, it was difficult not to believe that he had made it for us and only us.

24 LIFE WITHOUT TIMUSH

The day finally came for Timush to report. He sent us another letter telling us how much he would miss us and wishing us all the luck in the days ahead. We once again thanked him for everything he had done for us and told him we'd pray for him and his safety and health. We told him we would wait eagerly for his return and the day when we could all share another meal without the horrors of war and genocide looming over us.

The days that followed his departure seemed as normal as all the months before. The food continued to come regularly and our waste hoisted out as usual. The bell rang just like always to alert us of Hania's presence to carry out these tasks. If there was any special thing we needed to be made aware of she was always faithful to write to us. One of those times, she let us know that her brother was there more often to help her with the chores of caring for us. Of course, he had helped build the bunker and constructed the furniture for it so we were not concerned. We were grateful that he could be there to help her so that she didn't bear it all upon herself. And we were more than willing to do a small task he asked of us in return. For example, he would send his tobacco down to us so that we could cut it up for him, no doubt a tedious task he did not enjoy.

But after a few weeks passed we began to sense Hania's weariness in continuing her promised duties. She began to ask for more money for the food and supplies. It was much more than Timush had ever asked and we began to worry that perhaps she was burning out. Mendel still had some money to fulfil her demands but it wouldn't last long at this rate. Would it last until we could come out of the bunker? And if not, would she abandon us as a result? Timush's absence was becoming a great worry to us. She had never been as fully committed to our survival as he had been. And then there was her potential suspicion about Timush and Tusia. The uncertainty of the situation caused our anguish to grow more and more each day.

In the meantime, a very welcome letter arrived from Timush to Hania. She shared it with us and we couldn't wait to read it. The letter was addressed only to her but in it he cryptically referenced 'the children,' asking how they were and telling her to give them his greetings. He didn't want to mention us directly for fear of the letter being discovered. But we knew who these children were. He let us know that all was okay for him, even though he was very near the front lines. He wished us well and hoped that we were also okay. In the letter he placed a photo of himself dressed smartly in a German uniform. It pained us to see him in this outfit that we had come to despise. But we were glad to see him safe and sound.

More weeks passed and Hania's lack of resolve in continuing to hide us became more evident. Her punctuality in bringing us food and other needs fluctuated greatly and the amount and quality of it was also inconsistent. Finally, she confirmed her uncertainty with a letter to us. In it she wrote that she was becoming increasingly fearful that we would all be discovered. She suggested that we should make plans to leave the bunker soon because she didn't think she could bear the pressure of the responsibility much longer.

Even though we had anticipated and expected this for some time, seeing the words in her letter stunned us. The thought of leaving to face the horrors that surely waited outside terrified us. We had grown so secure and comfortable we didn't know if we would have the strength or will to survive as we had before.

We did our best to convince her to continue hiding us. We appealed to her sense of heroism and the reward she would obtain after this was all over. But it seemed nothing we wrote could reassure her, and in subsequent letters she continued to pressure us to leave. She was afraid that the war might go on for years and in that scenario, it would be impossible for her to sustain the help. She didn't think she could last many more weeks, much less several years if it came to that.

Indeed, her fears were rational. Hania had kept up Timush's practice of providing us with newspapers and other accounts of the war. We had continued to track the progress of the war on a map he had provided us for that purpose. It was early 1944 and both in Italy and on the Russian front the lines of battle had stagnated. It would be months before the Allies would land at Normandy, and of course we had no knowledge that such an attack was even being planned. So, there wasn't much hope that an end to this terrible war would come anytime soon. But we continued to plead with her to give us more time and finally offered to leave by April if the situation in the war didn't change.

A few weeks later, we began to notice that the house above us had been completely silent for many days. There had been no letter or message from Hania telling us she was going away. The long silence and days without any sign from her began to make us frantic. But we calmed each other, telling ourselves there could be scores of reasons for the delay.

Then one evening around ten a letter descended down the flue. We jumped toward it and opened it not knowing what to expect. The words in the letter were frightening. Hania explained that her brother had suddenly become hysterical. She was fearful that he was losing his mind and going completely mad. He was behaving totally irrational and speaking nonsense. But what she wrote next terrified us the most. In one of his rants, he had threatened to go to the Gestapo and tell them about the bunker and us hiding inside. Hania was panic-stricken and didn't know what to do. For all she knew he had already reported this to the authorities and they may already be on their way. She now insisted that we leave the bunker as soon as possible and that there was no time to delay. We had to be out before dawn.

New terror began to fill our minds. Leaving the bunker would be certain death but staying in it with this new threat looming over us seemed intolerable. Would it not be better to get out and at least face our destiny rather than sit inside burdened by this great uncertainty? We debated frantically the best course of action but we couldn't come to an agreement. Tusia and Mendel wanted to wait it out, but Edek and I felt it was best to take our chances on the outside. We felt there would be many more options for us out of the bunker than being trapped inside it. The hours passed and we still hadn't come to a decision. Some of us prayed while others could only weep. I was stunned and numb. We had survived so narrowly so many times before. The possibility that our luck might finally be ending paralyzed me.

As morning began to dawn, we finally agreed that we must prepare to leave. Just as we began to gather a few things, we heard footsteps above in the house. Fear gripped us as we heard them ascend up to the attic. Who was this and what was next for us? Then suddenly a letter dropped down through the flue. Even though we didn't yet know what was in the letter, the sight of it alone was a great relief. We grabbed the letter and ripped it open. It was from Hania. She wrote, "My dears, my brother has just committed suicide. He hung himself in the stable. I am very sad, but God's will has been done. Surely, He has spoken. He has taken one life for five."

The words brought tears to all of our eyes. Once again we had been miraculously saved. That it had come by such tragedy for Hania was heartbreaking for us, but she had accepted it as God's will and her resolve to continue to provide for us returned. From then on, Hania never again pressured us to leave the bunker and her efforts to supply food and the other needs never waned.

A few weeks later some German army officers and soldiers retreating from the Russian front came to the house and demanded to be housed there for a few days. There wasn't much Hania could do and protesting too much might have aroused their suspicions. But after surviving the diligent search by the Jewish policeman, she felt confident we wouldn't be found. So, the German soldiers settled in and made themselves at home. We were not sure how many of them there were but they made plenty of noise while there. Even though we too were confident that they couldn't find the bunker, the heavy footsteps, loud voices and banter were unnerving. We waited anxiously for them to leave.

Then one night, the officers decided to build a fire in the fireplace. They asked Hania to help them prepare it. Hania became very fearful for us since in all the time we had been in the bunker they had never used the fireplace. She didn't know if the smoke would descend down the flue and suffocate us. She ran up into the attic and quickly sent a message down to us. Now we were petrified for we had never thought about what would happen in this event.

We could hear the wood being stacked onto the hearth and the cracking of the kindling as they prepared to light the fire. We waited nervously as the flames took hold above and the fire began to crackle and sizzle. What would we do if the smoke began to fill the bunker? Would it be best to just sit there and asphyxiate? Or would it be better to pull the stone out and give ourselves up to the

Germans. Either way seemed certain death for us, so the futility of our decision was choosing which was the most painless way to die.

As the flames grew bigger, we kept a close watch on the flue. To our great relief and delight, there was no smoke coming down into the bunker. In fact, the stream of fresh air actually seemed stronger. Our nerves calmed quickly and we breathed a huge sigh of relief. We settled back into our normal routine but stayed even more diligent to keep the noise down. As long as the soldiers were in the house, Hania couldn't send us food and we couldn't empty our waste. So naturally we hoped they would be leaving very soon. Finally, after a couple of days, Hania notified us that they had gone and once again our spirits were lifted and our confidence boosted, knowing that the bunker had remained undetected.

25 "THE RUSSIANS HAVE ARRIVED!"

The occupation of the house by the German soldiers would not be a solitary event. In the days and weeks that followed, troops fleeing the Russian advance westward came through Tluste. Several times more, Hania's house was commandeered to house these soldiers. The retreat by the Germans was a very welcome sign of things to come, but each time they occupied the house we hunkered down in fear that one of them might discover our hiding place.

During these occupations we stayed completely still and silent—afraid that the least movement might be detected and suspicions aroused. Staying still wasn't all that difficult, since we had been in so many situations over the past few years in which we had to exercise this control. But no matter how adept we were at becoming living statues, when one of us felt the urge to cough or sneeze, the fear of doing so made it even more difficult to suppress. The mind can play tricks on a person, and at times thinking consciously about not coughing or sneezing can quickly bring on that urge. Knowing you cannot cough or clear the throat can invoke a sensation that you're being smothered. Fortunately, we always managed to stifle these involuntary functions during these visits.

As more weeks passed, the news that the Germans were in full retreat gave us great hope that our ordeal might be over soon. It was now mid-March 1944. We had been in the bunker for almost nine months! There's no question that was a long time, but the actual experience of it seemed much longer. For us, it felt as though it had been years. And no doubt the ordeal had taken years off of our lives. We hadn't eaten a fruit or vegetable in all those months and any meat or protein was also scarce. We hadn't bathed properly or kept up proper dental hygiene. My teeth were rotting and falling out. My skin was potted and scarred from scratching the rashes that plagued me. Exercise was very limited in such a tiny space so our muscles were atrophied. The bunker had kept us from being killed by the Nazi murderers but, if the war didn't end soon, it might eventually be our cause of death because of the appalling living conditions there. We waited—hopeful, but haunted by the fear that relief might not come soon enough.

As the next few days passed, noise from outside the bunker intensified. As the Germans retreated, tanks and motorcades of military personnel shook the ground. Shouting and gunfire were occasionally heard and we knew that the battle had arrived. But we had no knowledge of what the chaos ensuing above us meant. Were the Germans being pushed back? Were the Russians arriving and winning? Would there be further stalemates along the front, once again delaying the end of the war?

Hania couldn't tell us because, fearing for her safety, she had left the house to go and stay with her mother until the turmoil settled down. We didn't know how long she would be gone, but before leaving she had faithfully made sure we were well provided for. She had sent down several days' worth of food for us. Being there alone, so far underground with no communication or help from above was harrowing. But we waited and listened for any clues about what was happening above.

Then on March 22, 1944, a day none of us will ever forget, something terrifying happened. While we sat listening intently to the continued rumblings from the world outside, suddenly a huge explosion rocked the house above us violently. The bunker shook like it was at the epicenter of an earthquake. The wooden beams cracked and dust and dirt rained down on us. Our kerosene lamp went completely dark and we could taste soot pouring into the room from the flues. Then more explosions jolted us but these were farther away fortunately, and didn't cause any more damage to our hiding place. It was clear that a battle was raging outside and a bomb or mortar shell had hit the house. We huddled together in fear, not knowing whether this would be our last day alive. Would the bunker finally become our tomb as the bombs buried us alive? The fear and uncertainty we felt then are impossible to convey in words.

The battle drew on throughout the day and well into the night. Finally, in the early morning hours of March 23, all became quiet. We were able to relax once again and breathe a sigh of relief. We were still alive and the bunker was still intact. The dust and soot had settled down and the draft from the flues had cleared the air so we could breathe easily. Now we waited in a silence almost as deafening as the bombs and rumbling of the armies had been. The anticipation built as the hours passed without any indication or communication from above.

Suddenly we heard the door of the house swing open and footsteps run across the floor. The footsteps darted up the stairs and into the attic. Then a most welcome and familiar voice shouted down to us, "The Russians have arrived! The Russians have arrived!" It was Hania and with great joy and delight she shouted down to us once again, "You can come out now!"

It is impossible to find the words to describe what we felt at that moment. We had been buried underground for nine long months and now it was finally safe to come out. Joy, relief, elation, jubilance, ecstasy—none of these words alone can fully describe the end to our long nightmare. And even all these words together cannot sum up what we felt. But mixed with all of those feelings was the overwhelming sadness that would always remain for our lost family members and friends and the destruction of our entire lives and the Jewish community.

The war had been raging for almost four years and I would soon be sixteen years old. Some of the most formative years of my life had been taken from me as I passed from a young boy to a teenager. It wasn't easy to process all of this in the moment, especially alongside the natural fear of what we might have to face once we were back in the outside world. The worst might have been over, but our struggle to survive was not.

26 OUT OF THE BUNKER

After her jubilant announcement to us through the chimney flues, Hania quickly descended down the stairs to the cellar and tossed aside the sacks of potatoes that hid the opening to the bunker. She tapped hard upon the face of the stone that covered it and shouted to us to help her pull it out. With a hammer and chisel she chipped away at the mortar and plaster that held the large rock in place. From the inside we jostled the stone up and down to help loosen it from the wall. We pushed hard on it with the pole Timush had given us for just this purpose. Slowly the stone began to move forward and out of its hole. The adrenaline building up in us from the excitement of knowing we would soon be free fuelled our effort and soon the rock shot out across the cellar floor.

One by one we pushed through the opening and into the basement. There we saw a disturbing sight. Sunlight penetrated down into the room from the floors above. One of the bombs had hit the house squarely and it was severely damaged. Miraculously all three floors were still standing and the stairs were in place—but only barely. We suddenly realized how close we had come to being disintegrated by the powerful explosion. This was just one more narrow escape to add to our long list of incredible deliverances.

But now wasn't the time to stop to reflect on the past—we had to get out fast and determine the next steps required for survival. It was late March, but it was still very cold, and our clothes were tattered and threadbare and unsuitable to the weather. Hania found some old clothes and blankets and gave them to us to wrap around ourselves. We carefully ascended the rickety stairs and made our way outside. The relatively low light inside the basement had already been difficult for us to get used to after having been inside the dark bunker for so many months. Once outside, the bright white snow that completely covered the ground intensified the glaring midday sun. Our eyes were blinded by it and filled with moisture as the pain of the glare forced them closed.

We stood outside with Hania and looked back at the house. We marveled at how it could still be standing and how close we had come to being buried alive. The wind howled all around us and we knew we had to move on to find food and shelter and news about the war. We started walking toward the main road and Hania walked with us. When we reached it, she stopped and said to us, "Goodbye and I wish you the best. Go find the Soviets and stay with them, and you should be safe." We turned to her and thanked her for all she had done for us and for the risk she had taken to keep us alive. Then we each gave her a hug after which she walked back toward the house.

So many questions overwhelmed us now. The safety and security of the bunker was now behind us and we had no idea what dangers lay ahead. The fear of being discovered by the Germans was gone, but another fear beset us. Where would we go? Where would we live? What would we find to eat? And perhaps worst of all, was the war really over and would the Nazis return?

We started walking toward Tluste and soon we came across a small unit of Soviet soldiers. As soon as we saw them, we started running toward them and waving to them. As we got closer, we could see that they were in terrible condition. Their uniforms were worn and dirty. Their vehicles were rusted out and full of dents. The men were pale and gaunt with unshaven faces and disheveled hair. We wondered out loud to each other, "Were these the forces that defeated the magnificently disciplined German soldiers?" The sight of these troops was a drastic contrast to the memories we had of the perfectly outfitted and polished German soldiers. How could it have happened?

As we approached them, they stopped suddenly as if in surprise. They looked down at us and one of them asked, "Who are you? Where did you come from?" We replied back with some jubilation, "We are Jews. We are Jews and we survived!" Perhaps naively, we expected them to share a bit of the joy in our triumphant announcement. But their reaction made the blood run cold through our veins. "What? Why the hell didn't Hitler kill you too? We have been traveling for hundreds of miles, all the way from Odessa, and we have not seen one Jew the entire time." Their reaction was disheartening and put us on edge about what we might face now under the Soviets.

It was clear that these Russian soldiers couldn't care less what happened to us under the Nazis and they had no interest in giving us any help. So, we quickly moved on toward the town. On the way we met a few other survivors. There hadn't been many, but like us they had miraculously escaped death. Some had been hidden in nearby villages or in the countryside. Others had come from the same work camp where my aunt had been before Timush found her.

Mendel's sister had been one of those who had been hidden at a local farm not too far from Tluste. She had survived with her husband, her cousin, a ten-year-old girl and a six-year-old boy. This was also a miracle. It was very rare for such a young boy to survive in hiding. So often at that age they didn't fully understand the danger they faced and the pressure of remaining quiet. In cramped spaces, the ordeal became too difficult for them. As a result, those who were willing to hide Jews would refuse to hide young children for fear the attempt would end in disaster. We heard many horrifying stories of parents who were forced to kill their own children when the noise they made threatened to reveal their hiding place. It was a terrible decision forced upon people in desperate circumstances. In these cases, the parents were hiding with others whose lives would also be endangered if the noise revealed the hiding place. It became a choice between one person dying and everyone dying. These occurrences may be the most insidious consequence of what the Nazis wrought upon our people.

We met up with Mendel's sister not too long after we arrived back in Tluste. She came there at the same time as other survivors were arriving. I am unsure exactly how many, but there may have been 20 or 30 people in all. We were somewhat surprised there were any left, but considering that, before the war, Tluste had thousands of Jews, the number didn't offer us much comfort.

As the survivors came into the town, we looked for familiar faces hoping for friends to be among them. Suddenly I saw my good friend Sam coming towards me. He spotted me too, and in an instant, he was running as fast as he could to hug me. We met and grabbed each other and jubilantly hugged each other. We could hardly speak because of the overpowering emotion that gripped us. But we finally did and we sat down to recount our tales of survival. Sam was one of those who had been in the work camp. In everything he told me, one thing in particular stuck in my mind: Sam said that to keep clean and to avoid being infested with lice, he had bathed himself frequently with snow. He had always shown ample street smarts and a natural talent for survival, and I believe he survived largely due to those skills. It was such great relief to see him again and see that he had also escaped. He had risked his life a couple of years earlier to save mine and now to see him alive gave me great joy.

Now that we had arrived, we went back to our old neighborhood. On the way we saw dead bodies in the street. Some of them I recognized, including one of my brother's friends. It was a horrible sight and the memory of it is etched forever in my mind. The buildings around us were almost completely destroyed and everything that wasn't nailed down in them had been looted out. We went to our house and to my grandfather's bakery, to see if they were still there. But they too were almost obliterated and offered barely any shelter from the cold. We scrounged for food wherever we could, but there was almost nothing to be found. Luckily, we found a few potatoes and begged some bread from some of the local peasants.

The memories of all the tragedy we had faced there were very painful, and we didn't want to stay. But we had nowhere else to go so we settled in there for the time being. Sadly, however, like a vivid recurring nightmare, the pattern would start over: it wouldn't be long before we'd be uprooted and, on the run, again.

27 THE GERMANS RETURN

On top of the angst created by hunger and exposure to the elements, a new fear came down upon us with a heavy reality. Rumors arose and spread quickly that the Germans had mounted a successful counter attack and were on their way back to Tluste. Nothing could have been more devastating to our morale than this news. After all we had survived, would the monsters come back and finally succeed in the objective to do us all in?

It wasn't long before the rumors were confirmed and we saw that the Russian troops had begun to retreat to the east. The survivors debated what to do next. Even though for most this had been their home for generations, there wasn't much left here to hold onto. Only memories—many years of good ones and just a few short years of the most horrific ones. For us, those last years were enough to convince us there was no need to stay here and take the risk of being captured and killed. We decided we would flee with the Red Army and do everything we could to stay behind the Russian line.

Most of the other survivors decided to flee to the east as well. However, some of them made plans to hide again and wait it out one more time. Mendel's sister was one of these, and she tried to convince us to stay with her. "Look, if you go with the Russians the weather and the cold will do you in. Come with us and we'll hide with the man who hid us. He is a very good man and he will protect us." But we were adamantly opposed to the idea. Tusia quickly told her, "There is no way I am going to stay in a place where the Germans have control. I cannot go back into a bunker or any other hiding place again and I *will* not go back to be hidden by any Gentiles."

We wasted no more time in debating our next move. The Russians were retreating fast, and we set out to go with them, obliged to walk for lack of any other means of transportation. We started down the road with the goal of getting to the next major town to the east, Czortkow, which was almost 15 miles from Tluste. In normal conditions a walk of that distance would not have been a major feat. But we had very little clothing and what we did have was not suited for the cold and snow that surrounded us. Our shoes were almost completely worn down and offered little shield from the wet and muddy ground. Nevertheless, we had no other choice, so we marched on with the scores of others fleeing Tluste.

As we walked, Russian troops lumbered past us in their big trucks and their convoys. It was very clear they were on the run. Hundreds of them moved quickly past us toward the east to escape the German army. We struggled through the mud and snow with resolve, knowing that the Germans would soon be on our heels and they would show no mercy.

Finally, we reached Czortkow and found ourselves in the center of the town in a big public square. There were a few other Jews gathering there who were also intent on getting far away from the German hordes. On one side of the square was a large, stately building. It served as the main post office for the town. The building had a large staircase leading up to its front door. There on the steps stood some Russian soldiers and several Red Army officers. One of them stood out and had the air of great importance about him. His uniform was in much better condition that the other Russian soldiers we had encountered and it was draped with dozens of medals.

As we approached the steps, one of the Russian officers saw us and called out to us, "Hey there, who are you and where are you going?" Tusia answered telling him we were Jews from Tluste that had survived and were now fleeing the German advance. He motioned us to come up to him and said, "Well the Germans are still advancing so you must keep fleeing to the east."

We were surprised because he was now speaking to us in Yiddish. It turned out that he was also Jewish and an officer in the Red Army. Then the highly decorated officer came down the steps toward us and started to speak to us in Russian. The Jewish officer turned to us and, again in Yiddish, said, "Do you know who this man is?" We shook our heads and then he continued, "This is General Zhukov." The name meant nothing to us, but after the war we learned how important this man was. He became renowned for his service during World War II and would eventually be named Supreme Commander of the Soviet Army. Zhukov would join the top commanders from the U.S. and Britain, Generals Eisenhower and Montgomery, in Berlin for the signing of the German Instrument of Surrender, which officially ended the war in Europe.

The General also wanted to know who we were and where we were going. We told him who we were and that we were fleeing the German advance. We then said that we would like to go with his troops so as not to be captured and killed by the Germans. He said, "I don't know. Everything is confusing and we don't know if we will have to retreat again from the Germans." Then he turned and walked back to the top of the steps.

The Jewish officer repeated his advice for us to continue to flee. But then he looked down and saw that Tusia had no shoes, only sackcloth wrapped around her feet and tied up with string. Then he looked sympathetically at us and said, "But why should you walk? Why don't you climb onto one of our tanks there and ride with them as they retreat?" We didn't need any more cajoling to accept his offer and we bounded toward the tank and jumped onto it.

The tank was a part of a large convoy of military vehicles retreating from the German advance. The weather was bitterly cold and we were sitting on the gangway along the side of the tank trying our best not to be knocked off by the bumpy ride. The huge machine lumbered slowly down the muddy road with us clinging to the top. Soon it started snowing again. The snow intensified and very quickly we found ourselves in a blinding blizzard. The tanks moved slower now but the blizzard didn't bring them to a halt. We were covered with snow and were freezing but we held on tightly preferring the difficult ride rather than a more difficult walk.

We clung to the tank with the snow still falling heavy all around us. Eventually the convoy stopped for a short while. We debated whether we should continue on with them not knowing how far they would retreat. Would they have to fall back behind the Russian border? If so, that might expose us to a new set of dangers. At this point in the war the Soviets didn't have full control and authority in the Ukraine, so the tight control of people that existed in Russia wasn't fully in force here. But we knew that once we crossed the border circumstances could change and we might not ever get out. On the other hand, if we stayed here with the Germans coming in full force to regain the territory, we may be risking our death once again.

Eventually the ride on the tank became so tiring that we began to consider walking again rather than endure the pounding. Perhaps going on foot might be less agonizing after all. Either way, we were going to be in pain and discomfort but the difficulty of hanging on to the tank on the bumpy road seemed more difficult to us now. We jumped off the snow-covered tank and down to the ground. As we did, we felt excruciating and stinging pain on our hands. We had been so cold from head to toe that we didn't notice the bare skin of our hands had fused to the ice-cold metal on the tank. When we jumped off so quickly, the frozen skin was ripped off of our palms and the delicate tissue underneath was laid open and bleeding. We had experienced so many aches, pains, cuts and bruises through our long ordeal that fortunately I have long forgotten most of them. But the pain of that moment for some reason is etched in my memory.

From there we started walking again, away from where the Germans were advancing. This took us to the north and east away from Czortkow. The roads were in terrible condition and filled with a dirty, slushy mixture of mud and snow. What shoes remained were riddled with holes and worn to their last bits of leather—and as the Russian officer had noticed, my sister wore only sackcloth on her feet. Every step took concentrated effort to make and we stumbled and fell often. I found some old clothes and ripped them up into strips of cloth and tied them around my shoes to help insulate my feet. But now the snow was knee deep all around and in no time my feet were soaked through. After a while, they were completely numb and I could barely stand.

We were walking with a group of people who were all moving away from the front lines. I was happy to find that my good friend Sam was part of this band of refugees. We didn't walk together, but saw each other at various points along the way. I would have loved to stay with him for the journey, but it was all I could do to stay with my family. I was getting so tired and cold that I began to fall behind everyone. Edek and Tusia dropped back to help me every so often, taking me by the hand and pulling me along. They urged me to keep going and not give up. It took every ounce of willpower to keep putting one foot in front of the other. When I hear the cliché "one step at a time" or "one foot in front of the other," I think back to that arduous journey and the words become more than just a figure of speech.

That evening we entered the town of Kopeczynce to the northeast of Czortkow, where we came upon an abandoned house that we hoped would give us shelter from the cold. Once inside, however, we realized it would be only a slight improvement over being outside. The house had been almost completely stripped of anything useful by looters. Some broken chairs lay in one corner and trash was strewn all around. Many of the cupboards in the kitchen had their doors stripped off and there was not a scrap or crumb of food to be seen. But the roof and walls gave some relief from the wet and cold, but the gaps and cracks in them let in the freezing draft. Despite all this, we settled down for the evening and tried to sleep.

Even though we were completely exhausted and weak, sleep did not come easily. There were no beds, so we slept on the hard floor with nothing to cushion our weary joints and bones. The frigid air that slashed across our waterlogged clothes and shoes constantly nettled us out of slumber. But we did manage a few broken hours of rest and soon the morning came.

When we awoke, we heard sobbing coming from one of the other rooms. We moved toward the cries and peeked into the dark space just inside the door. There on the floor a teenage girl knelt over the body of her younger sister. She rocked back and forth, head in her hands, weeping softly but uncontrollably. The girl was gripped with grief and couldn't speak. The little girl she knelt over was not much older than seven or eight years. She lay there completely still and not breathing, her skin a ghostly white. Her eyes were partly open and stared eerily upward at nothing. She had frozen to death in the middle of the night. What cruel twists and turns of emotions this nightmare brought upon so many. What despair her sister must have felt upon finding her lifeless. A few days earlier they must have been so joyous knowing they had miraculously survived the terror from the Nazi murderers. And now, liberated and filled with the promise of better days, hope was painfully snatched away.

We watched as she began to pull herself together and suppress her tears. She bent over and kissed her sister gently on the cheek and lightly stroked her hair. Then slowly she raised the little girl's body to a sitting position and began to pull the dead girl's arms out of the sweater she was wearing. Once it was off, she lowered her again and closed her eyes and gave her one more kiss. Then she stood up, wrapped the sweater around herself and left the room.

This wasn't the first time we had seen the hand of death and its vicious reality up close. But this was a very tragic vignette to observe and a stark reminder that just because we were no longer under the Nazis, the battle for our survival was not yet won.

28   DELIRIOUS WITH FEVER

There was little time to consider the tragedy we had just witnessed
and no time to mourn with the young girl or help her bury her
sister. Such were the times of this horrifying ordeal and another
part of the dehumanization Jews faced. The Germans were
advancing still and we needed to be on our way as soon as possible.
So we began our walking journey again, desperate to make sure we
got as far away as possible from the approaching front line.

We kept moving northeast toward the town of Podwoloczysk.
Along the way, I began to feel achy and started to tremble with
chills. This time the cold I felt wasn't from the freezing weather but
from a fever that was taking over my body. I marched on but felt I
would collapse at any moment. I could tell my temperature was
rising to a dangerous level fast. Great relief came later that
afternoon when we found another abandoned house to stop and
rest for the night. We were just outside of Podwoloczysk and very
close now to the Russian border.

I collapsed on the floor inside the house and curled up into a fetal
position to try and warm myself from the chills that spread over me.

Edek knew right away what caused my sudden illness. It was typhus.

Typhus is caused by lice and, with the squalid conditions Jews faced in their ghettos, work camps and in hiding, it didn't take long for the pests to spread rapidly. When I was in the work camp at Lisowce, I kept a close watch on my body to look for them. I became very good at finding them and I have a graphic memory of crushing them with my fingers until I felt them pop. While in the bunker, we didn't have a problem with lice, as we did our best to keep clean and were essentially quarantined from the infestations of others. But since we had come out of hiding, we had been in close proximity to survivors who carried the bugs with them. All of us now were crawling with them, and I had fallen victim to the terrible disease they carried.

At first Edek showed no signs of sickness and he felt normal. But Tusia was also beginning to feel a fever coming on. So Edek sprang into action and took off to ask some nearby Soviet soldiers for help. He wasn't sure that they could do much to help but, in his desperation, he told them of our plight. To his great relief, the soldiers took him to one of the medics who gave him some medicine to treat us. He rushed back to us with the pills as fast as he could. I'm not sure what kind of medicine he brought, but it was certainly not a cure, since the only treatment for typhus was a vaccine. Nevertheless, the medicine did help lessen the pain and reduce the fever.

Edek remembered well how the disease had consumed our father and vowed to do everything he could to keep us from the same fate. One of the most gruesome effects of typhus is a strange black fungus that often grows on the tongue of the victims. If it isn't cleaned off and controlled it will eventually overtake the mouth and airways and suffocate the person. Still etched deeply in our memories was the image of the fungus growing thick in our father's mouth and how he struggled to breathe. Fear gripped me as I realized I might soon be consumed by it too.

But confusion and befuddlement soon overtook my fear. I began to hallucinate as my fever climbed ever higher. It wasn't long before my awareness of what was happening became very dim. When I try to remember those couple of days it is mostly a blur. But I do remember vividly lying on the floor in the abandoned house beneath one of the windows. I remember hearing in the distance the fighting that was beginning to approach us. The Germans were conducting air raids ahead of their advance and the bombs were dropping in the town nearby. Every now and then bright flashes of light filled the sky outside and lit up the room where I lay. The Russians were shooting flares into the night to help them spot the attacking aircraft.

There was no furniture in this house and we had no blankets or any other type of bedding to pull over us. So, I lay there half frozen on the rigid planks of the floor. I don't think I even had anything on which to rest my head. I do remember being in pain and shivering and that overshadowed the discomfort of the hard surface.

Tusia now was also engulfed with fever and struggling to fight it off. Edek focused his steady attention on both of us. He had been able to get a little bit of sugar and salt along with some clean rags. He soaked the rags and wrapped them around a small stick then dipped them in the sugar and salt. He used the new made tool to wipe down our tongues and remove the fungus that was beginning to grow on them. He stayed vigilant to keep our mouths clean and our airways clear. Without his efforts we may very well have died in that abandoned house.

Soon I recovered from the fever and passed any danger of dying from typhus. But the effects of the illness had left me incredibly weak. I didn't have the strength to stand or walk and I couldn't speak at all. Edek kept up his care for me and every day when the sun was out, he would carry me on his back outside to make sure I got a good dose of fresh air and sunshine. In a few more days my strength began to return.

Why Edek hadn't come down with typhus yet was a mystery, but he would eventually succumb just as we had. By that time, however, Tusia and I had recovered enough to take over and help him, and we had been in Podwoloczysk for a couple of weeks and had gotten to know some people in the region. We learned there was a hospital, and with the help of a local Jewish doctor whose name was Schmeterling, we were able to get him admitted to it. There he would be cared for much better.

Tusia and I were able to stay at the hospital during Edek's confinement there. The staff gave us a place to sleep in one of the waiting rooms, along with some blankets and pillows to make us more comfortable. We still didn't have a bed, but at least we were in a warm, dry place for the first time in weeks. I did my best to stay close to Edek and help him as he had helped me. He had begun to hallucinate and sometimes became frantic, reacting violently to the imaginings that plagued him. Once, he thought there were bombs dropping all around him in the hospital and he cried out in fear. But I did what I could to calm him at those times.

29 THE NAZIS FINALLY
PUSHED BACK

Keeping track of time was one of the least of our concerns during those first few months outside the bunker. Daily survival was paramount, and in some ways those days seemed to pass rapidly. In other ways, however, they were like an eternity. This long after the events, it's difficult for me to piece together an exact timeline for our journey from Tluste to Podwoloczysk. But historical accounts show that it was late May of 1944 when the Germans retreated again. Our reaction to hearing the news at the time was one of great relief that we wouldn't have to cross the Russian border.

Once we learned of the retreat, we were reassured that it was safe to return to areas that were more familiar to us than Podwoloczysk. There was nothing really for us to go back to in Tluste, but we knew people in Czortkow and since it was the center of the region we thought it held more promise for us. So, we made the decision to return there.

I hadn't seen Mendel since we arrived in Podwoloczysk. During our trek there he usually walked at the front of the pack and didn't stay with us. I am not sure why, but perhaps he wanted to lead the group in the direction that he preferred rather than just follow blindly. Now that we had recovered from our sickness and were ready to return to more familiar ground, we learned that Mendel had already made the decision to go back to Tluste and look for his sister and her family. We found out later the sad fate they had suffered. The family that had hidden them during the Nazi occupation was not happy to see them again. In fact, they, along with several of their neighbors, brutally murdered the whole family, hacking them to death with shovels and picks. Their decision to go back into hiding turned out to be a tragic mistake.

We don't know what caused this drastic change in the people who had once been their protectors, but most likely they had hidden them before only for the money they were given to do so. It had not been a gesture of altruism. Since Mendel's sister no longer had anything to pay them, they were ready to butcher them. We were shocked and mourned their deaths, but we couldn't help being very relieved we did not yield to their insistence that we join them. It was another twist of fate that had kept us alive.

The weather was now warmer, and the journey to Czortkow wouldn't be as difficult as the journey to Podwoloczysk. Even so, we weren't looking forward to walking all the way. There were plenty of Russian troops still moving back and forth along the road between the two cities, so we were able to get a combination of rides on the backs of their military trucks. Between those and the rides we were offered by locals pulling horse-drawn carriages of all types, we were able to get back to Czortkow much faster and easier than we could have expected. In just a few days we were back in the familiar town.

We soon met up with an old acquaintance from our days in Tarnopol, a Jewish man named Ginsberg. He had been a family friend before the war, and was now in Czortkow working with the Soviet authorities. He gave us a lot of help in getting settled. Through him we found an apartment that we shared with a

Russian agent. His name was Doroshenko and he was a member of the NKVD. He was as interesting and colorful a person, as one would expect, given his profession. We got to know him well, of course, and he occasionally helped us find food and other basic necessities of life.

The Germans were gone now from western Ukraine but things were still chaotic. Even though the Nazi regime's collapse was imminent, the war wasn't completely over in the West.

In June we heard the exciting and welcome announcement that the Allies had landed at Normandy. At that point, we couldn't know for certain that this invasion would be the beginning of the end, but we rejoiced at the news and sensed that the Nazis would soon be defeated. The Russians continued to march toward Berlin from the East but progress was slow for such a rag tag army. As a result, the Soviets were conscripting every able-bodied man to fight on that front. A lot of Jews were eager to join the ranks and go to fight their persecutors. But even those who were not were being forced into service. Edek had just turned 21, so he was a prime candidate. Needless to say, he wasn't eager to go and he was still weak from his bout with Typhus so he hoped for a way out.

We had known from the earlier Soviet occupation that the Russians had a great appreciation for art and music, and they put a great emphasis on supporting and preserving the arts. Edek was confident that if he could show them his talent as a violinist, there was a chance he might avoid being drafted. So, he sought out the local department in charge of theatre and music. He learned that there was a new group being formed to perform all kinds of theatre. The group would need musicians, actors, dancers and singers. Of course, he no longer had a violin, so he desperately searched everywhere for one. With some luck, he found one on the black market, purchased it and made plans to audition.

Unfortunately, when he arrived, he was informed that the group already had enough violin players and there was no need for any more. But he was told they were short of dancers and they asked if he could dance. Edek hadn't really been trained in dance, but he had loved to dance as a teenager and knew some ballroom style dances. He had also taught himself a few tap dance routines from watching Fred Astaire movies. So, with just the slightest nervous hesitation, he enthusiastically said yes. They set an audition for him the very next day.

There was very little time for him to brush up on his dance steps, but Edek mustered up all his confidence for the audition. When he arrived, a young, attractive woman who would be his judge greeted him. In the initial interview with her, he sensed that she was attracted to him. He hoped this would bode well for getting accepted.

When it was time for him to show his skills, Edek asked the pianist to play music for a fast foxtrot. He attacked the dance with all the vigor and passion he could muster, and from the subtle smile on the woman's face he thought he was doing pretty well.

But, when the song ended, she looked at him with an expression of amusement and, after a moment she asked, "Do you smoke?" Edek replied, "Yes." So, she pulled out two cigarettes and handed one to him. Then she lit them both. After a couple of puffs, she looked at him and said with a knowing smile, "You're not a professional dancer, are you?" Edek gazed back in embarrassment without answering. His spirits dropped at the thought that he had probably missed his chance. But then she continued, "No I didn't think so. However, I can see that you have a lot of talent. And you know the Western dances. I could use someone like that. I want to feature some of the more modern, popular dances—not just the folk dances we often do." Edek's heart leapt as he realized she was going to bring him into the troupe.

From that day on, he worked hard to learn all the dances and the athletic moves that were part of them. Eventually he became one of the best dancers in the troupe. He also got some small roles as an actor in the plays the troupe produced. Ironically, in one of them he had to play the part of a German soldier. He didn't have any speaking lines but was an extra on stage.

The sight of him in a German uniform was unsettling, and I remember it vividly today. But the important thing was that he had escaped going to the front. Later we learned that two of Edek's friends, who were his age, had gone to fight—and both of them had been killed in the war. It was another a tragic instance of Jews miraculously surviving the genocide only to lose their lives just when they thought the worst was over.

After settling in Czortkow, we felt safer and safer every day, as the horrors of our ordeal seemed to be over. Tusia and Mendel began to plan for their long life together and they married not long after we arrived.

For me, I was ready to seize the day and turn our newfound optimism into success. My many harrowing experiences over the past few years did nothing to destroy the typical teenage belief that I was invincible. In fact, my newfound freedom seemed to bolster it. The world was renewing and I was eager to find opportunities that came with that. I suppose I had inherited from my father the strong desire to create my own business. The thought of being in the employ of others did not appeal to me at all. It was through this lens that my eyes lit up when I found out that there was a place in a nearby city from which I could buy yeast at wholesale prices. Immediately the idea came to me that I could go there, purchase some and take it to Tarnopol to sell for a profit. So, I made my plans to leave as soon as possible and prepared to set out on the journey a few days later.

I told Doroshenko about my plans and somewhat surprisingly he encouraged me to carry it through. In fact, he made up some documents for me that would allow me to safely go on the trip without being harassed by the authorities. The city was Czernovic and it was just to the south of Czortkow. As I had done many times before, I chose to hitchhike. I was fortunate to catch a couple of rides and in a few hours I arrived safely. The city was large and very beautiful and escaped severe damage during the war. I strolled down its streets enjoying the busy shops and cafes. At the end of one street I turned the corner and suddenly in front of me was a movie theatre with its bright marquis advertising the latest Hollywood film. The name of the film was 'Sun Valley Serenade' starring Sonia Henie, Glenn Miller and his world-renowned band, and Milton Berle. I had no idea what the film was about but I was mesmerized by the thought of seeing it and suddenly I found myself at the box office buying a ticket.

The film was beautifully made and directed. The music was so powerful and almost brought me to tears. I was so overwhelmed by it that I bought another ticket and watched it again. The movie transported me to a world so distant and different from the horrific one I had experienced during the past few years. There could have been no better therapy. It filled me with hope and optimism that life could be good again.

I left the theatre on an emotional high and made my way to the yeast factory. I had brought with me a large suitcase to transport the bags of yeast carefully back. I purchased it and quickly made my way to the train station. I decided to return by train since the suitcase was now much heavier than on the trip there. But little did I know that would foil my attempt at entrepreneurship. The journey was going well until the train approached Tarnopol. As the train slowed to enter the station, suddenly NKVD agents began to move through the cars checking for papers from the passengers. I heard their loud calls demanding people to show proof they were traveling legally. Fear gripped me as I realized that Doroshenko had given me the necessary documents to get me to Czernovic but not to make the journey to Tarnopol.

Without a moment's hesitation, I dropped the suitcase of yeast onto the floor and kicked it under the seat directly opposite me. I would be in enough trouble once they discovered I did not have the proper documentation. But having a suitcase filled with evidence of my capitalistic plans would certainly land me much deeper. Within seconds, the NKVD agents were in my compartment and standing over me. I presented the papers Doroshenko had created. They looked them over and immediately they knew they were not in order. They demanded that I come with them and kept me close as they finished their rounds through the rest of the cars.

When the train arrived in Tarnopol they escorted me to a room inside the station. As I approached the room, I was surprised to see a man from Tluste that I recognized. He also recognized me and waved to me as they took me inside. Inside there were other passengers who had been arrested for various reasons. On the opposite side of the room was another young boy and I decided to go sit down on the floor beside him. It was close to another door that was open and unguarded. I thought perhaps I might find an opportunity to slip away and out if I could position myself close enough to it.

I was there for several hours just waiting. No one came to interrogate me and we were not being told anything about how we would be processed. Then an officer came into the room and looked over toward me and the other boy. He called out to us but it was unclear which of us he was addressing. The boy pointed at himself and looked inquisitive as if asking, "Do you want me?" The officer shook his head and the boy got up and went toward him. As he did the officer turned his back toward us to engage another detainee. At that moment I knew he could not see me, so I quickly rolled over onto all fours and scampered out the open door. Fortunately, on the other side, it opened up into an empty hallway and I darted down it and out into the main station. I had slipped out completely unnoticed! There was not a moment to spare however, so I quickly found the exit and within seconds I was free and out onto the streets of Tarnopol.

But what now? Where would I go and how could I get back to Czortków? It had been a long time since I had been in Tarnopol but I remembered the name of a man whose sister used to work for my father. I thought hard and my memory brought back the name of the street and the general direction of where he lived. I set out for the area but the city had been bombed extensively and much of it was still in rubble. As a result, I found it difficult to navigate with so many buildings destroyed. But with great determination, I wandered back and forth through the neighborhood, hunting down street after street until I eventually I found his house. It too had been badly damaged but to my great delight, he still lived there. He welcomed me to stay until I felt it was safe to attempt the trip back home. My first attempt at entrepreneurship had failed and once again I had narrowly escaped a difficult situation.

The next day I began hitchhiking back to Czortków. Soon after I returned, I learned that my friend Sam was now living in the nearby town of Borschow. It was some distance, but we got together as often as we could and our friendship deepened. One day, the two of us decided to visit Tluste and see what had become of it. I wasn't really very keen on going back, as there were not many good memories for me there. But Sam had grown up in the town and his family had been there for a long time, so out of respect for him I agreed to go. I suppose because of those bad memories I don't remember much about that day or what we saw or did there. But it was a pivotal moment for Sam and I think the last time he ever visited his birthplace.

Sometime later, I learned that our NKVD roommate, Doroshenko, was going to Sam's town for a mission. When he told me he was going, I asked if I get a ride with him to go see my friend, and he agreed to take me. Some of his missions were raids on the Banderowcy, the same group of Ukrainian Nationalists that Timush had considered joining instead of fighting with the Germans. As an intelligence agent, it was his responsibility to seek them out and arrest or kill them. It was a dangerous job and he used to joke with us about it when we were together in the apartment. He would say, "Today there is Doroshenko, but tomorrow maybe, no more Doroshenko." And then he would laugh with a loud bellow. He would get us to say it with him and, like a dark nursery rhyme, we'd recite it in rhythm together and all laugh.

But for Doroshenko the thought was a real threat and no laughing matter. His prophecy would soon come true and I came very close to being a part of it. When the time came to leave with him for Borschow, I couldn't find him anywhere. I don't know if he had already left, was simply late, or whether I had gotten the departure time wrong. Whatever the reason, I ended up not going with him.

That night Doroshenko didn't return to the apartment. Initially, we didn't think much about his absence because his schedule was often erratic. But after several days had passed and he still hadn't returned, we began to wonder what had happened to him. We would soon learn that on a mission just a few days before, he had been ambushed and killed by some Ukrainian nationalists. Had I gone with him that day, there is a good chance I would have been killed too. Another lucky twist of fate had kept me alive.

As I noted earlier, the fact that the Germans had left the area did not mean we were in complete safety. But as a young teenager, who had survived so many brushes with death, I suppose I felt a bit invincible. All young people feel that way to a certain extent, even in normal times. But my experiences had made me fearless, probably beyond the point of wisdom. I had another friend in Kopychyntsi, the town where we had stayed overnight when fleeing the final German advance. One day I decided to visit him. It wasn't all that far away, but the only way to get there was by walking or hitchhiking. The road was heavily trafficked, busy with cars, trucks, military vehicles and even horse and buggies. Because chaos was still prevalent, it could be a dangerous journey—and even without counting the danger, it was impossible to predict how long it might take, especially if the other travelers along the way were not inclined to offer rides.

I started out on the day's journey and made it in good time to Kopychyntsi by hitchhiking. The Russians had a curfew in place all over the region so I planned to stay overnight with my friend so we could have more time together. Otherwise I would have had to set out on the return journey too early. The next day, we were enjoying being together so much that we soon lost track of the time. It was getting very late in the day and I realized that I was going to be hard pressed to make it back to Czortkow before the Russian-imposed curfew. I hurried down the road and started hitchhiking. As it turned out, however, I had to walk most of the way back and didn't make it into Czortkow until after the curfew hour.

As I was walking down the street toward our apartment, two Russian soldiers suddenly rounded the corner. They saw me and approached, ordering me to stop. They asked me for my papers, but since I didn't have any, they immediately suspected that I might be a spy for one of the underground movements. They told me I was under arrest and told me to turn around with my back facing them. They each had rifles with bayonets on the barrels and one of them put the point of his into my back and ordered me to get moving. They marched me down the street toward their headquarters.

Eventually we arrived at a historic castle that had been built at the founding of the city hundreds of years earlier. This served as their command post. The buildings were very old, but big and impressive as they sat on a hill overlooking the center of town. Once inside, one of the officers took me to a dark office and shoved me down into a chair in the middle of the room. Then he walked out. By now I was very frightened and didn't know what they might do to me. I sat and waited alone for about an hour—but in my anxious state it seemed much longer.

Finally, the officer returned with a bright light and shone it directly into my eyes. Then he began to shout questions at me. It seems humorous to describe such a cliché scene, and it may be hard to believe interrogations with a bright light in a dark room actually occurred. But I lived through one and can verify that at least this once, they did. It was an effective fear tactic used by authorities to intimidate and extract information from captives. For me at the time, it was no laughing matter—I was consumed by fear and ready to tell him everything.

After a couple of forceful questions, the officer told me to empty my pockets and place everything on a nearby table. I didn't have much on me, but for some reason I had brought the Morse code book that my brother and I had used in the bunker. I pulled it out and placed it on the table. Immediately he grabbed it and said suspiciously, "Aha! What is this?" Why would a teenager need to know Morse code? Probably the only reason would be if he were assisting some kind of fighting force. And if that were the case, it was most likely that I was a part of one of the nationalist movements resisting the Communist government.

I did my best to explain to him why I had it, relating the full story of being in the bunker and wanting to talk to my brother without Mendel hearing us. At first, he was skeptical and continued to press me harder under the bright light. Time after time he made me repeat my story, hoping some inconsistencies would expose me. But since it was the truth, I never faltered. My fear grew with each question shouted at me, but I kept as cool as I could and maintained my innocence. Eventually he took a break from his inquest and left the room.

I waited for at least another hour, perhaps two, before he finally returned. He came into the room and switched off the bright light. Then he told me that he believed my story. But he wasn't quite done with me yet. He had some more questions. Now his focus turned to finding out information about Ukrainian Nationalists in Tluste. He pressed me to tell them about anyone I knew there that had been part of the movements for Ukrainian independence or those who had collaborated with the Nazis. I was relieved that I was no longer their target but his method of interrogation was still frightening. I was more than willing to assist him with this information, especially about Nazi collaborators. But it wasn't easy for me to remember many of them, even though he intensified his effort to get as much information from me as possible.

The interrogation went on through the night and well into the wee hours of the morning. I think it was around three o'clock before he finally stopped. Finally, he was convinced I was not a threat and that there was no more information I could give him about potential enemies in Tluste. A few minutes after he left the room, a female soldier entered and took me to another room. She pointed to a cot and explained I could sleep there until the curfew was over in the morning.

I was extremely exhausted and glad to have a place to lie down, but I was still unnerved by the ordeal and couldn't sleep. I lay on the bed eagerly waiting for dawn. Finally, the morning light broke through the window, signaling the curfew was over. I jumped up, put on my shoes and bolted for the door to make my way home. My brother and sister were somewhat surprised to see me so early in the morning. They hadn't been worried at my absence, simply assuming I had stayed overnight with my friend in Kopychyntsi. But when I told them my story, they were happy that I had escaped yet another dangerous situation.

30 TIMUSH AND HANIA'S FATE

My ordeal with the Soviet soldiers had been desperately frightening, but I felt some satisfaction from helping them with information about some of the Nazi collaborators in Tluste, especially one in particular. I don't remember everyone I told them about, but I do remember mentioning Schap, the Ukrainian policeman who had caught me coming home from trying to find food and had struck me hard against the face.

Since we had returned to Czortkow we had renewed contact with Hania to see how she was doing. Like most, she was surviving with only the barest of essentials. And she was still intricately involved with the push for an independent Ukraine. We had no idea at the time, but she was working with the Banderowcy. We were eager to hear news about Timush so we tried to see her as often as possible. She told us he was still alive but had deserted the German army after being wounded. Now he was in hiding trying to recover so he could get back home. But he needed help to get some basic things in order to stay alive. She asked us to help her get food, clothing, shoes, and bandages for his wounds. Every time she would come to Czortkow to see us she brought a list of things that she asked us to help provide for him. We were more than happy to assist, so eager to and filled with hope that we would see Timush again. We scrounged together money to help her buy some of those things and also searched hard to find the ones we couldn't purchase.

Hania continued to visit us on a regular basis with requests for supplies for Timush. We were always eager to hear any news from her about how he was doing. However, the news she brought was always very general and with very little detail, as if she didn't really know much—or perhaps just didn't want us to know. Even though we thought this a bit strange, we trusted her and certainly didn't want to deny Timush anything that he might need to survive his ordeal.

In April of 1945 the Soviets announced that former Polish citizens living in the Ukraine would be allowed to return to Poland. The border between Poland and the Ukraine had shifted many times over the previous two centuries and Poles and Ukrainians were intermingled there. Ethnic tension between Russians, Ukrainians and Poles had been a recurring problem for hundreds of years in the border region. As the war ended in the region, ethnic strife began to build again, especially among the Polish and Ukrainian nationalists. They often clashed, and several incidents of massacres on both sides are well documented. The Soviets were eager to squelch this conflict and the patriotism that accompanied it. As a result, they offered former Polish citizens inside the newly drawn Ukrainian border the opportunity to immigrate to Poland. Many Poles, including many of the surviving Polish Jews, jumped at the chance.

For almost two decades before World War II, the cities where we had lived, Tarnopol, Czortkow and Tluste, were within the borders of Poland. We had always been Polish citizens and considered ourselves Polish in nationality. But now the Soviets—in agreement with the Allies—had moved the Ukrainian border westward and all of those places were now within the Soviet Union. The announcement that we could leave was a welcome one. We remembered the suffocating hand the Soviets had dealt us financially when they seized our father's business. We certainly didn't want to live under them again, and felt the best opportunity for us was in the West.

We wasted little time preparing to go. Even though the region had been the only home we had known, it had no nostalgic hold on us anymore. We were leaving nothing behind, other than the frightening memories of the torture and genocide. But we were concerned for Hania and set out to find her before we left. We knew she hated the Russians and since we considered her family, we wanted to help her get out of the country. We did not know it at the time but she was helping the Ukrainian Nationalist movements. As a result, she was in greater danger than we knew. She could become a target of the Soviets and killed or captured as they tightened their grip on the country. Edek came up with an idea that would allow her to go with us. He suggested to her that she pose as his wife so that she could get permission to leave as well. Once safely in Poland he assured her they could divorce and she would be free to go her own way.

Edek soon found her and made his proposition. But Hania was very dedicated to her patriotic mission and refused. Many years after the war we learned the reasons why. Not only had she been helping the nationalists, but she also had been having an affair with a man who was in the movement. Exactly how long the affair had been going on, we didn't know, but we suspect in hindsight that it was occurring even while we were in the bunker. She would hold onto her convictions and dedication to her lover at the cost of her life. They were eventually captured by the Soviets, given a mock trial and executed by hanging.

At the same time, we learned that Timush had died fighting on the front lines of the war many months before we left Czortkow. All of the supplies Hania had extracted from us were, in fact, not for

Timush at all. They had been for the fighters in the Ukrainian resistance. It was a bit disheartening to learn this, but we felt no ill will toward her, only respect and honor.

While she was not very enthusiastic about helping us to survive, she had worked very hard to comply with Timush's wishes—and in so doing put herself at great risk. And her ultimate goal of a free and independent Ukraine was a noble one for which she gave her life. Many years later Hania was recognized as a Ukrainian hero for her efforts. There is now a plaque in her honor of her and Timush in the center of town in Tluste for their service to the nationalist cause.

As for Timush, we wept for him when we learned of his death. We longed to know what had happened and how his life had come to an end. But there was very little information to be found about those last chaotic days of the German army. How we wished he had survived so we could have seen him again and brought him into our family. That is something we are convinced he wanted more than anything else. We ached to pay back—even if it could only be in some very small way—what he had sacrificed and given to us. We owed him our lives in so many ways.

31 THE SEARCH FOR A NEW HOME

April of 1945 was a chaotic and unsettled time throughout the world, but especially so in Europe and for Eastern European Jews who had survived the Holocaust. Millions of people were on the move in all directions across the continent trying to build new lives out of the destruction that war had brought. And though the end of the war was very close, it wasn't yet completely over. The Soviets were making their final push from the East to Berlin and the Allies were moving in quickly from the West. Most knew Hitler and the Nazi regime would soon fall. But amidst that optimism, there was still great uncertainty about the future.

It was against that backdrop that we made our plans to take advantage of the Soviet offer for Poles to repatriate. Now that Hania had made her decision to stay, there was no reason for us to wait any longer. We had little time to plan our trip and determining exactly where to go wasn't an easy decision. As far as we knew at the time, we had no acquaintances in western Poland.

We grabbed only what we could carry with us and set out for the train station. Thousands of Polish citizens had already descended on the rail yard by the time we arrived. There were not enough trains arriving and departing to keep the masses moving consistently out of the terminal, so the crowd of refugees grew by the hour. We checked the schedules of the passenger trains on their way westward and realized all of the trains heading that way were fully booked for several days. Many people had given up waiting for passenger trains to get out of the city and were beginning to crowd into the cars of freight trains. We decided we had no desire to camp out at the train station waiting for a suitable passenger train. And times were so uncertain, we were concerned that the Soviets might rescind their offer as quickly as they had made it.

We decided our best option was to take one of the freight trains. We asked around among our fellow evacuees and some of the people working in the station to see whether we could figure out which trains were bound for the West. Eventually we identified one and climbed aboard a boxcar that was already filling with people. By the time the train began to move we were packed in tightly with dozens of other fleeing Poles.

The only thing we knew when we hopped on board is that the train was bound for Poland. But we soon learned that its final destination was Krakow. We also heard that Krakow had escaped the massive destruction that so many other cities in Eastern Europe had experienced. Now that we knew where we were going, we allowed a glimmer of hope and optimism to soothe a small part of our anxiety.

We had no idea how long the journey would take. The railcar was open at the top and there was no comfortable place to sit or sleep. The ride was terribly rough and the car lurched from side to side like a boat on choppy waters. But we settled in and looked forward to the trip's end. The train moved along at vastly different speeds depending on its scheduled pickups and deliveries. At times we sat motionless for what seemed like hours. At other times we sped down the track at full speed. When it pulled into a train yard we often moved back and forth around the various tracks as cars were hitched and unhitched. The entire experience was a combination of monotony and nervous anxiety from the uncertainty of what might come next.

Hours passed and we were getting closer to Krakow. We pulled into a small station in a town called by a name I no longer remember. But I do remember the scene there very well. As the train arrived, people along the platforms were huddled around newspapers talking about the headlines that spread across them. President Roosevelt had died and the world was mourning the loss of a great leader who had risen to the occasion during the most difficult time in human history. I had lost track of time in the last few days. Even today I am still unsure about exactly when we left Czortkow. But it was April 12, 1945 when we pulled into that station. The date of the American president's death is the only way I have to give our journey context in time.

At the end of a very long day we arrived in Krakow, where we were finally able to get out of the cramped and dirty boxcar. Jumping down, we made our way to the terminal. I had never seen a train station so big. Rows and rows of tracks and platforms spread across the rail yard from the main terminal. There was an underground tunnel that allowed passengers to safely cross between each platform. These are common now in even smaller train stations but for me this was a new sight. Once inside the terminal, my eyes opened wide to take in the massive space rising up to an elaborate ceiling many feet above us. I knew now that I was in a much different world than Tluste. For me Tarnopol was a big city, but here the entire world seemed to open up in front of me.

As we made our way out of the station and into the streets of Krakow, my excitement began to build. Its cafes and shops were coming to life again after the long and lean years of war. Big stately buildings rose above the sidewalks and vendors sold all kinds of food and wares on the corners and in the squares. The hustle and bustle of the city was invigorating for me. For the first time in a long time, I felt the hope that life could be good again.

32 HOW TO SURVIVE IN KRAKOW

Krakow had captured my heart and imagination in every way. Life in a small village like Tluste had its advantages for sure, but for a teenager aching to become a young man, life in the city was intoxicating. And Krakow had intrigued me for as long as I can remember. As a young boy in Tarnopol I remember sitting by the radio listening to hours of programming coming from all over Europe. But one broadcast in particular was special to me and even today it brings back very pleasant memories.

Every day at noon we tuned into a radio station from Krakow to hear the daily ritual of Saint Mary's Trumpet Call. In Polish it was known as *Hejnał Mariacki*, or 'Saint Mary's Dawn.' It is a signal from the tower of Saint Mary's Church in Krakow played by a trumpeter every hour on the hour. It is a short and solemn melody lasting less than a minute. But it is played four times in succession as the trumpeter sounds it out in the four cardinal directions of East, West, North and South.

No one is quite sure exactly when or how the tradition got started but it has been one that has lasted for over six hundred years. It wasn't uncommon for such signals to be played in the many walled Medieval European cities when they opened and closed their gates, so it's possible that's the origin. Strangely, the melody of Saint Mary's trumpet call ends abruptly in the middle of a melodic phrase. Legend has that once, when the city was under attack, the trumpeter played his signal to warn of the approaching enemy. His call saved the city, as they were able to close the gates before the hordes arrived, but unfortunately the bugler was shot directly in his throat by the attacking army just at the point in the song where it ends now.

After arriving in Krakow, we were so consumed with trying to find ways to survive that the memory of the Saint Mary's Trumpet Call was the last thing on my mind. I had forgotten about it completely and neither the knowledge that we were headed there on the train nor the eventual arrival in the city brought it back to me. But the next day after we arrived, we went into the town center and to the markets that abounded there. We were searching hard for any way to make a few zlotys to buy food and to pay for a place where we could live.

Then suddenly, as we moved quickly through the city streets on our quest, the first few notes of the melody rang out over the buildings and echoed through the alleyways. I stopped in my tracks and strained hard to listen. At first, I was confused. How could I recognize such a familiar sound in such an unfamiliar place? But like the voice of an old friend it called to me and my heart leapt with joy. It only took a few more seconds for me to remember. I was transported back to our warm and comfortable apartment in Tarnopol, sitting on the floor cross-legged gazing into the speaker of our Telefunken radio. The melody went on and stopped, then played three more times just as I had remembered. The music gave me a great sense of rejuvenation and hope. Once again I believed that life could return to normal and that the dark days we had experienced were finally behind us.

Events moved quickly for all of us once in Krakow. Only a couple of days passed before we saw some friends from Czortkow who had also fled the Russian-controlled Ukraine. After so many terrible experiences, survivors developed a heightened sense of the importance of helping one another. Our friends had been there long enough to find a place to live. When they found out we didn't have a home yet, they immediately invited us to stay with them until we could find one of our own.

Now that we had a place to anchor, we sought out ways to make money. All across the city people were selling anything they had to make money for the basics. On every street corner one could buy used clothing, shoes, jewelry, pots and pans, cooking utensils and even furniture.

Generally, these were desperate individuals needing cash quickly to feed themselves and their families. So, the asking prices reflected that reality. But in the larger markets many of the same wares were being sold at higher prices. It occurred to us that there was an opportunity for profit if we could sell these goods there. We scraped together a few zlotys and began to comb the town for things we thought could be resold. I was lucky to find some very nice fabric and I was able to sell it for a good profit. Before long we were leveraging this idea into a living. It wasn't much but it was keeping us fed. And as we got better at recognizing which items brought the best return, we gradually increased our fortune. Tusia was able to get a job in a local office, although I can't remember exactly where now. Our income was slowly but steadily growing and eventually we were able to get an apartment of our own.

My newfound optimism in Krakow was not unfounded but we would soon learn that antisemitism wasn't dead in Poland. The large influx of people from the repatriation was deeply resented in some areas and there were fears that the Jews would demand the return of property that had been stolen from them during the Nazi occupation. As more and more Jews came from the East, tensions grew. Stories of attacks on Jews by Poles began to proliferate.

Indeed, during the first few years after the war, Poland had more than its share of such violence. Fortunately, however, for the most part it wasn't organized but rather seemed to be isolated events brought on by local tension. Nevertheless, there were several events that seemed frighteningly reminiscent of the akcia we had faced under the Nazis. In these, scores of Jews were killed. History even records them as pogroms since they were clearly carried out by angry mobs. Krakow wasn't a place for a lot of violence against Jews but in certain places we were not welcome and it wasn't uncommon to be greeted with a racial slur. Perhaps Tusia saw it more than any of us because she worked closely alongside Poles in her office. To state it mildly, many of her coworkers resented her and were not at all hesitant to let her know their dislike of Jewish people. Insults and nasty epithets were thrown her way throughout each day.

Despite the tension we felt as Jews, life still seemed to be getting better for us. I felt very much at home in Krakow, and I loved the bustling atmosphere of this Western-influenced city. The shops and cafes were full every day and music was playing everywhere it seemed. I was enjoying my new 'business life' and the satisfaction that buying and selling could bring. But I was still young, and the big city had given me a thirst for seeing more of the world. In another chance meeting I had reconnected with a close friend of mine from Czortkow. We had met there after the war, and I had discovered that, like me, he had survived by hiding. His name was Lolek Berkowicz and he had survived along with his father and sister. I was thrilled to find he had come to Krakow too. Once we found each other, we began to spend almost all our free time together and became even closer friends.

One day Lolek came to me and said, "How would you like to go to Prague with me?" My ears perked up immediately—it sounded like the sort of adventure any seventeen-year-old would relish. He told me that he had an aunt who lived there and he wanted to go see her. Of course, the lure of exploring another cosmopolitan city was probably the greater attraction for him. For me it was the only reason to go and without any hesitation I replied, "Yes, I'll go with you. There is nothing holding me here in Krakow."

33 A CIRCUITOUS ROUTE TO PRAGUE

Paradoxically, traveling from city to city in the aftermath of such a great conflict was both easy and extremely difficult. The easy part was the transportation: there was very little stopping one from just jumping on a train—whether passenger or freight—to head anywhere one might wish. The authorities lacked resources to patrol the railways for ticketless travelers or for those hopping freight trains. They were occupied with the greater priorities of rebuilding. The difficult part was that so many rail lines had suffered extensive damage during the war, so there were not many direct routes left between the major cities. Determining how to get from Krakow to Prague wasn't as simple as exploring an official timetable. In fact, no such thing probably existed, at least, not in any accurate form. On top of that, the authorities were still trying their best to control the movement across borders and we knew we would need some paperwork to exit Poland and enter Czechoslovakia.

The Allies had anticipated the massive number of refugees and immigrants that were moving in all directions across Europe. In 1943 they established a forerunner to the United Nations known as the United Nations Relief and Rehabilitation Agency (UNRRA). Even before the war's end, this agency began planning how to manage the disorder that would be left behind after the tight controls of the Nazi regime were gone. To prevent total chaos, certain parameters had to be met in order for refugees to obtain the documentation needed for crossing borders.

Strangely, Krakow didn't have an UNRRA office. The closest one was in the nearby smaller city of Katowice. A few days before we were to leave, we arrived at the agency to get our papers. Once we made our request the official asked us which concentration camp had held us as prisoners. Lolek and I looked at each other in confusion. We had both been hidden and were never in a concentration camp. I turned to the officer and said, "We were not in a camp. We were hidden. And I was in a forced labor camp." The officer stayed quiet for a few seconds and then he repeated his question, "I'm sorry. You may have misunderstood me. I will ask you again. In which concentration camp were you prisoners?" Now we were even more confused and had no idea how to answer. Finally, the officer said, "Oh, I see. You were in Bunzlau? OK. I will process your papers now."

Then the message the man was trying to convey to us sank in. Because of the UNRRA rules we had to have been in a concentration camp in order to be approved for travel to Czechoslovakia. We were lucky that we had encountered such a sympathetic official who was ready to accommodate us in spite of the restrictions that had been put in place. But from then on in my travels, if I was asked, I always told people that I was a survivor of the Bunzlau Concentration Camp.

Now that Lolek and I had our papers we were eager to get started for Prague. I grabbed just a few belongings and put them in a sack. I said farewell to my brother and sister and to Mendel. We met at the train station the next day to figure out which train would get us to our destination. It wasn't an easy task. As I noted earlier, there were no direct routes any longer between Krakow and Prague because of the destruction of so many bridges and rail lines during the war. Prague is exactly due west of Krakow, a straight shot of less than 250 miles if one could travel as the crow flies. The journey today by train between the two cities is only a six- or seven-hour trip. Before the war it may have been a little longer than that, but probably not by much and it certainly could have been completed in less than a day. However, we soon learned that we'd have to go south to Budapest first and there we'd have to catch another train to Prague. But getting to Budapest was also not a direct route. We had to first go to Kosice in Slovakia and from there to Bratislava and then on to Budapest. It was a circuitous route that more than quadrupled the distance of our trip. In terms of time, it was probably at least ten times longer. And little did we know when we started out, that we would have a frightening encounter that would delay us even further.

We boarded the train to Kosice in Krakow. It was a passenger train but there was no conductor or station master checking for tickets. The train was almost full when we stepped on board and hundreds more were squeezing into it. Every compartment was packed and people stood in the corridors and along the gangways. We found a spot in a crowded compartment and pushed our way in to settle down for the long journey. The train sped away into the night and it felt good to be on our way. We arrived in Kosice without any difficulty and waited for the next train to Bratislava. A few hours later, we were on our way again. By the time we arrived in Bratislava, we had spent a whole day traveling. Once again, we had to change trains for Budapest and this one was more crowded than the other two. To say we were like sardines would be an understatement, but somehow, we found a compartment with just enough room for us to wedge ourselves into.

We breathed a sigh of relief as the cars lurched and slowly moved out of the station towards Hungary. But our sense of relief would be broken soon enough. As we approached the next station, we looked out to see hundreds of Russian soldiers crowded onto the platform. The train pulled to a stop and within a few minutes an officer from among them was making his way down the corridor shouting, "Everyone out! Everyone out now! We are taking over the train!" Our hearts sank as we watched them forcing all of the passengers out onto the platform and the soldiers taking over the compartments. We were pushed along in the flow of humanity struggling to comply with the demand. Stumbling off of the gangway we looked up and saw that many of the former passengers were scurrying up the sides of the cars and onto the top of the train. Lolek looked at me and said, "We could ride up there too!" I quickly agreed and we found a ladder and bolted up to the top.

34 ANOTHER BRUSH WITH DEATH

The train was an electric train and that put us in a precarious position once we ascended the car. The cables and hardware to power the train were all around us connecting to the wire above that provided the electricity. Maneuvering around these high voltage objects was tricky but we eventually found an empty spot in which to crouch down. It wasn't long before the train started moving again and we quickly realized that we'd be best lying completely flat since the overhead cabling dipped and moved as we went forward. It wasn't very comfortable, but we had been in much worse conditions over the history of our quest to survive the Nazi regime and before long we were adjusted and able to relax.

The sun began to dip down below the horizon as we sped on toward Budapest. The night seemed to come much quicker than usual perhaps because we were still a bit nervous about keeping our balance atop the cars in the coming darkness. Soon it was pitch black and the far away lights from nearby farms and villages did nothing to illuminate the objects whizzing by. Sparks flashed and popped above us in a regular rhythm as the pantographs pushed up against the contact wire. From those flashes we got a brief look at the dozens of bodies all stretched out across the roof of the car. It was an eerie sight and brought back frightful memories of the dead bodies stretched out in the streets of Tluste after we left the bunker. But I fought those thoughts off and tried to let the steady rocking of the train lull me to sleep.

As difficult as it was to sleep, I soon found myself in a state of semi-slumber. Half conscious of the steady movement of the train and the frequent sounding of its whistle, the other half of my mind was drifting into the strange world of dreams. But soon I would be wide awake and confronting another danger. I awoke to hear two Russian soldiers speaking to each other. It was in quiet tones at first and I couldn't understand what they were saying. The voices caused me to remember my frightening experience being interrogated by the Russian soldiers in Czortkow. But it was very dark and I couldn't see their faces. Then suddenly a bright light flashed in my eyes. Then the light moved away from me. They were shining their flashlight on Lolek. The voices grew louder and then into a full shout.

"Znimaj sapogy! Ja ubiu tebia kak sobako," the loud voice said in Russian. I understood the words, "Take off your boots or I will kill you like a dog!" The men had come up to the roof of the train to see what they could steal from the passengers and had spotted Lolek's new riding boots. They were beautiful brown and knee high. The leather still shone brightly even after all our travels. Now these two decided they were going to take them from him. Once again, the shout rang out, "Take off your boots now!"

Lolek stayed quiet and said nothing. He pulled up into a sitting position and grabbed his knees in a defensive stance. The soldier again shouted at him to take off his boots, but Lolek just shook his head and refused. "Take off your boots or I will kill you like a dog!" he screamed. The second soldier reached down and grabbed Lolek by the shoulders and shoved him flat to the ground. Then he sat down on his chest and held his arms to the roof of the train. The first soldier then grabbed Lolek's feet and tried with all his might to pull off the boots. But they wouldn't budge. He pulled as hard as he could but Lolek cramped his toes tightly into the soles so that his feet were wedged solidly inside. The soldier started shouting again, "Take them off or I will kill you like a dog!" He continued to pull but Lolek was able to keep the boots from sliding off even the slightest bit. The soldier screamed again, "I'll kill you like a dog! I'll kill you like a dog!"

Suddenly a Soviet officer who had heard the ruckus appeared on the ladder and quickly climbed onto the roof. He shone his flashlight toward the shouting and said, "What's going on up here? What is all this noise and shouting?"

When the soldiers heard this they immediately jumped up and ran the opposite direction from the officer. Then they scampered down a ladder and into one of the cars. The officer shone his light on us and not seeing any signs of disturbance turned and went back down inside the train.

We had survived this attack for now but we began to worry that the soldiers would return again to demand the boots. They might even make good on their threat to kill us. We didn't think they would be foiled a second time, so we decided that we should get off the train as soon as an opportunity presented itself. In a few minutes the train started to slow and soon after was barely creeping along. We agreed that this was our chance, so we quickly moved to the edge and down one of the ladders along the side of the train. Then we leapt into the darkness and tumbled down the embankment alongside the rails. We were scuffed up a bit but not hurt, fortunately. As we got up and dusted ourselves off, we started walking in the same direction as the train.

35 THE SLOW TRAIN TO BUDAPEST

We had no idea where we were and it was pitch black, which made walking very difficult. Stumbling often, we nevertheless tried our best to keep up a good pace. Eventually we saw the lights of a small train station in the distance. With renewed energy, we walked as fast as we could toward it. The closer we got to the station the more we could see that this was a tiny stop along the route. Three tracks split the short and narrow platforms. A small building that wasn't much bigger than a wood shed stood on one side. When we finally reached it and went inside, we saw that it only took one man to take care of everything. He was the stationmaster, the ticket salesperson, the signal operator and probably the janitor too. We were glad to be at a station, but also realized that most trains passing through did exactly that—passed through—without stopping. What kind of luck would we have catching another train to Prague here?

We approached the lonely man behind the counter and asked if he could tell us whether any trains stopping here would get us to Czechoslovakia. His answer was not very encouraging. "There are not many passenger trains that stop here. And nothing directly to Czechoslovakia I'm afraid. But there are some freight trains that will stop here in the next few hours. You can jump on them and wherever they go, that's where you'll go." He spoke to me in Slovakian, but the language is very close to Polish so I was able to understand him.

We didn't have many options at this point, so we decided to take his advice rather than sit for hours—or perhaps days—waiting for a passenger train. So, we went outside and sat on a bench to wait. Finally, still for a few minutes, it was the first time I was able to reflect on the encounter with the Russian soldiers. So, I asked Lolek, "What were you thinking? Why didn't you just give them your boots? You could have been killed! We both could have been killed!" He looked at me and said, "It wasn't just the boots I was afraid of losing." He pointed down the bottoms of his feet and whispered, "I have some silver coins stashed away in them. My father gave them to me. It's a lot of money to lose and I thought it was best to take my chances. It's all I have." I smiled at him and he chuckled slightly. Then we both burst into laughter. The relief that we felt after surviving one more brush with death had turned into a strange elation. We sat back on the bench and relaxed, and began to appreciate the quiet night.

I must have dozed off for a while, even though it was not a very relaxing sleep, because it seemed like only minutes before a freight train crept into the station. However, when I looked up at the station clock, I saw that several hours had passed. The train wasn't stopping, but it was moving so slowly we were pretty certain that we could jump on it without much trouble. So, we jumped up and began to run to the end of the platform. There we jumped down beside the track and got our speed up to match that of the rail cars. We found a foothold on one of them, grabbed a handhold, and scampered up and over into the open bin. We were on and we were moving, but where to was anyone's guess.

We lay down and tried to rest. Soon the morning light began to reveal the countryside around us. We still didn't know where we were going but we would eventually find out that we were heading away from Prague and instead toward Budapest. It was a major city and surely there we could find a train back to Czechoslovakia.

The train was moving at full speed now and day was arriving fast. We felt good and were hopeful that we'd soon be at a city where we could determine a way to complete our journey. But the fast pace didn't last long. The train slowed again below walking speed. We hoped that it would pick up to full speed shortly, but this didn't happen. We continued to crawl along, hour after hour. Occasionally we'd pick up speed. But just as suddenly, the train would slow again. We began to accept the reality that this was as fast as this train was going to run and we'd have to be patient. In any case, it was better than walking so we settled in for the long ride.

We had been on the train for a full day when it pulled into a small station. This station was bigger than the one where we hopped the train, but it still didn't look promising for catching a train to Prague, so we decided to stay on the freight car. As I surveyed the platforms and station buildings, I noticed a vendor selling fruit. He had a beautiful mound of dark, red cherries piled up high on his cart. The sun's rays sparkled off the polished skins and made my mouth begin to water. I was so hungry I had to have some of them. The train came to a full stop just as we neared the platform. I immediately jumped down from the car and ran to the vendor. I gave him a few rubles and he handed me a small basket full of the cherries. I was so hungry and the cherries were so deliciously sweet that within a few minutes I had devoured them all.

Back on the train with Lolek, we again started off at a slow pace. We were only a few miles down the track when I began to feel a sharp pain in my stomach. At first it was just a few twitches, which quickly dissipated, but before long, the pain became more constant. Suddenly I realized I wouldn't be able to hold my bowels. Now I was glad that the train was moving so slowly. I bounded down off the car and found a spot in the bushes just off the tracks. The cherries had been delicious for sure, but my stomach clearly didn't agree. Once relieved I got back on the train, which was still creeping along. I lay down and tried to relax but within a few minutes the urge to go again was upon me. Once again, I was off the train and into the bushes. It was a vicious case of diarrhea. For many miles down the track the routine of jumping on and off the train and into the bushes became a dismal ritual. Such a scenario would certainly have been entertaining in a Hollywood comedy. But for me at that time, it was no laughing matter.

I lost track of the passage of time while battling my stomach problem, but I think we had been on the train for two or three days before we began to see the outskirts of a large city. We soon learned that it was indeed Budapest. My stomach was better now but I was still queasy.

However, the excitement of reaching the city took my mind off of my nausea. We pulled into the main station and were very relieved to disembark the uncomfortable freight car. We ventured out into the city and once again the cosmopolitan atmosphere called to me and infused me with excitement. But we had very little money with which to enjoy it. We decided to see if there were any Jewish organizations in the city that might be offering assistance. Asking around, we met some other Jewish survivors who offered to help us. They gave us some food and invited us to stay with them for a few days. We decided to take them up on the offer since there was no hurry to get to Prague. We wanted to see some of this beautiful city while we had the chance.

36 FINALLY, PRAGUE!

For three days we stayed in Budapest and had a good time. Lolek enjoyed it too, but he was eager to get to Prague and see his aunt. He knew we'd have more support once we reached her. His aunt was Jewish of course, but she was married to a Gentile man who was a high official in the government there, and both of those circumstances had allowed her to escape any threat of harm during the war. It also helped that Prague had been a much more civilized place than Poland during the war, and there had been much less hatred and persecution of Jews. Because of her social status, Lolek was certain our time there would be much more enjoyable and advantageous than in Krakow or Budapest.

We found a train to Prague without any trouble and within a day we had arrived. There was one problem for us however. Lolek didn't know the exact address of his aunt's home. He did know the general area though, and we were able to find our way there from the main train station on Prague's excellent trolley system. We made our way to her neighborhood, which was known as Praha Nusle. From there we thought it might take some time to find her, and we were ready to fend for ourselves for a few days if necessary. But we would quickly get a pleasant surprise.

As soon as we were off the trolley, we walked just a little way up the street toward a grocery market. Outside, there was a group of women talking to each other in Czech. Lolek approached them and said, "Excuse me. By any chance do any of you know a woman named Bemova?" He spoke to them in Polish, but the Czech language is very similar, so they were able to understand him.

One of the ladies' mouths gaped open in surprise. It took her a few seconds to speak as she studied his face carefully. Then she said with great anticipation, "Lolek? Is that you?" Now Lolek was consumed by astonishment. He looked at her intently and suddenly his expression changed to one of great joy. He shouted, "Yes! It's me!" Then they grabbed each other in a strong embrace and kissed each other on the cheeks. Tears flowed down both of their faces as they continued to greet each other with broad smiles and laughter. Lolek then introduced me to his aunt and soon we were off to her home.

The apartment Lolek's aunt lived in was in one of the nicest areas of Prague. It was large and spacious and finely appointed with beautiful furniture and art. I had never been in a place so nice, even in my childhood in Tarnopol. She showed us our rooms and gave us some towels so that we could clean up after our long arduous journey. I knew that our time here was going to be special, but also that it probably wouldn't last forever—at least for me. And the Soviets were now in control here, which made me nervous about staying too long. Things were not under very tight control yet, but we anticipated that would happen soon enough. For now, however, I put aside any thought of the future and looked forward to a summer of adventure and fun in another beautiful European city.

Even though Lolek's aunt was fairly well to do and generous, we didn't want to take advantage of her, so we sought out ways to take care of ourselves as much as we could. We looked for places all over the city that were giving out free food or meals and took our lunches there often. We were touring all over the city every day. We visited every one of the historic places in Prague. We explored the many parks and gardens that abound there. The cafes and pubs were filled every night and the women were some of the most beautiful I have seen anywhere in my life. As young men, we couldn't have desired to be in a more vibrant and livelier place or one that appealed more to our newfound appreciation for life.

My time in Prague was a marvelous one for sure, but as the days passed, we could see that the Soviets were going to put more of a stranglehold on freedoms. Reluctantly, we decided it was time to make plans to leave. Where to go now was the question. We had heard that in Austria Jews were finding ways to immigrate to Palestine and, even though it was illegal at the time, there were organizations there arranging for the passage. The idea of going to Palestine where Jews had lived for thousands of years was appealing to me. And the adventure of trying to get there filled me with excitement, so I decided to take my chances in Austria.

37 FROM THE EAST TO THE WEST

Making the decision to leave Czechoslovakia was the easy part. Actually, getting out wouldn't be so easy. Restrictions for crossing the borders had been in place since the end of the war, but for a while they had been loosely enforced. Now as the infrastructure gradually improved, the border officials were strengthening their efforts in an attempt to control the massive migrations that were occurring. With the Soviets tightening their control over Czechoslovakia, we knew our chance of getting permission to cross into Austria was unlikely. We decided to get as close to the border as possible and figure out a way to cross undetected.

We made our way to the city of Pilsen, just east of the German border. We went to the train station and surveyed the situation there. There were too many officials watching and checking papers of the people going and coming. Once there we met other Jews who were also trying to get out of Czechoslovakia without papers. Some of them decided to go to the rail yards from which the freight trains departed. We decided to follow them and within a couple of hours we had jumped on a train that was southward bound towards Austria.

Once again, we were in for a long ride because of the slow speed of the freight train. It lumbered on toward the Austrian border, and with every lurch and shift of the cars our stomachs turned with anxiety. We had no idea what our fate would be once the train approached the border. Because of that, the day passed seemingly much slower than in reality. Finally, we were at the Austrian border and the train began to slow. We nervously waited for it to come to a full stop and for officials to begin checking the rail cars for stowaways. To our surprise, it didn't stop. It moved on past the border, eventually picking up speed again as we breathed a great sigh of relief and sat back enjoying the fresh summer breeze and the beautiful Austrian countryside.

A couple of hours passed and we could see we were approaching a small city. The tracks widened and we saw that we were entering a train depot. The cars slowed to a crawl as we came closer to the rail yard. Finally, it came to a full stop and many of the people on the train took the opportunity to get off to stretch their legs and look for something to eat. We decided to join them, not knowing how much further we might have to travel before finding a place to settle.

Most everyone on the train was a Jewish survivor from Eastern Europe, and this was their first time arriving in a territory that was solidly a part of the Third Reich. It wasn't long before we encountered some Austrians going about their business near the depot. We avoided them but a couple of other of our fellow passengers couldn't restrain their anger upon seeing them. They ran toward the Austrians and began to shout at them accusing of them of murder and genocide. Their pent-up bitterness had been primed to explode at anyone whose native language was German. Of course, the Austrians for the most part had been very willing participants in Hitler's maniacal plan to destroy the Jews and I certainly understood the emotional outbursts. But I knew that here and now was not the time to take revenge. We knew nothing about these particular people we had happened upon, nor their view of or history with the murderous regime. And even if we had, this was not the appropriate tactic.

Nevertheless, these surviving victims couldn't restrain themselves and they charged the unsuspecting Austrians and began to attack them violently. My friend and I, along with a few other passengers, decided it was time to intervene. We ran to the knot of brawlers and stepped into the middle of the slugs and punches being thrown, grabbing the attackers and pulling them back toward the train. The Austrians quickly ran away from the scene and reluctantly our fellow passengers began to calm themselves and regain their composure. Soon we were back on the train and moving southeastward toward the beautiful Austrian Alps. My friend and I felt a renewed sense of peace as we gazed toward the majestic mountainous skyline and we settled in for the next phase of the journey.

One of the other passengers who had helped us prevent the riot at the train depot came and sat beside us as we rode along. He was with his father and they had been the only members of their family that had survived. His name was Tomek Shoenfeld and we shared our terrible stories with one another. We became very good friends and have continued to stay in touch with each other ever since.

Soon the train was climbing up a steep incline in the midst of rocky hillsides escalating to sharp peaks capped with patches of snow. I had never seen mountains so dramatic in their landscape. The air was crisp and clean and invigorating. Occasionally we could see beautiful houses that clung to the slopes in defiance of gravity. Wildflowers covered grassy meadows between the rocky outcrops. The train rounded a bend and a vast open valley appeared in front of us with a crystal-clear blue lake gleaming in the sun. It was a beautiful sight like none I had ever seen before, and I was excited by the thought of being in Austria and getting to see some of its beauty.

Before long we began to approach another city. Some of the other passengers knew it was Salzburg and were aware that there was a major Displaced Persons Camp here, which was run by the Americans. As we moved through the Alpine valley toward the city center, we saw ever more beauty in every direction we turned. The mountaintops framed an area dotted with lovely houses and perfectly manicured gardens. Every sight, sound, and smell gave us hope for a new life and the promise of freedom. But little did we know that our days of imprisonment and restricted movement were not over even though we were now in an American controlled region.

When the train pulled to a stop in the Salzburg depot, American military police quickly positioned themselves all around it knowing that there would be refugees aboard. When we saw the armed men, our hearts sank and memories of the horror we had faced over the last five years rushed back. Even though we knew they were not our enemies, we also knew their job was to keep us from disembarking. Once again, we felt like prisoners.

We quickly learned that the DP camp was at full capacity and they couldn't let any more survivors into it. They were going to force the passengers aboard to keep moving westward. But no one could tell us where we eventually wind up if we stayed on the train. And our plan had been to go to Salzburg where we knew there were groups helping surviving Jews get to Palestine. So, we began to plan a way to get off the train unnoticed. We knew our best chance would be under cover of darkness, so we waited patiently for night to fall. It was late summer, so darkness didn't come fully until late. But even though we were eager to make our getaway, we knew it would be best to go after midnight when most people would be asleep and the surrounding streets mostly empty.

Midnight came and I, along with Lolek, my new friend Tomek, and his father, slowly and quietly climbed down off the train. Crouching underneath the rail car, we surveyed the area for any soldiers but could see none. Keeping as low as possible, we hurriedly made our way across the many tracks lining the train yard and ducked under cover behind a nearby platform. From there we carefully navigated our way around the outskirts of the depot and into the city streets. We had gotten away undetected. But we knew we had to keep moving. Our plan was to find the DP camp and see if we could somehow convince them to take us in. But we had no idea where it was.

Eventually we made our way to the center of Salzburg, and to our surprise, when we got to the main plaza, there was a group of others who had also escaped from the train that evening. They too were hoping to get to the DP camp. With all these people congregating in the middle of the night we were certain the authorities would soon notice us. We began to fear that we would be rounded up and placed back on the train. The group continued to grow over the next couple of hours and our anxiety grew with it. We knew we had to separate from this crowd and get to the camp quickly or we may miss our chance. So, the four of us decided to head out of town and do our best to find the camp on our own.

I don't remember how, but somehow, we got directions and found our way to the camp just as the morning light was beginning to fill the valley. We approached the gate with trepidation. The sight brought back some horrible memories: Fencing spread out in both directions from the gate to encircle the camp. Here an MP stood to keep people from going in or going out. I could only think about the irony of what we had been through, escaping camps that looked very much like this one, now believing we had been freed, only to still be at the mercy of those who guarded such places. How many more times would we have to endure being treated like common cattle, herded into corrals either by friend or foe? In my weary state from being awake all night my heart sank. But the thought of being turned away and forced back onto the train like livestock was also too much to bear.

As we approached the front of the camp the MP asked for our passes in order to enter. Of course, we had none so we sat down and waited, trying to determine what to do now. The sun was getting ever higher in the sky and we knew our time was limited. Should we try to go to another DP camp in the area or see if we could plead our case here with the officials? A few minutes passed and suddenly a man who looked like an official in the camp headed toward the gate. He ordered the soldiers to open it to let him out and he came over to us. He introduced himself and indeed, he was the man in charge of the entire camp. He also happened to be Jewish and he spoke several languages including very good English. Because of this the Americans had put him in charge.

After he told us who he was he said quietly, "You are Jewish. Would you like to come into the camp?" He was clearly speaking softly so the guards couldn't hear what he was saying to us. "Yes, please! We have nowhere else to go," we answered without hesitation. So, he continued, "OK. I am going to give each of you passes. But you must go away for a little while and then come back one at a time, not as a group. That way they will not be suspicious." So, we eagerly took the passes and thanked him. Even though he was in charge of the camp, perhaps he didn't have the full authority to admit people to the camp. But he could give passes for people to go out and come back in. We had come to just the right camp at just the right time. Once again, I had a remarkable stroke of luck in my long journey of survival.

The head of that camp became a lifelong friend of mine, along with his assistant who helped him run the camp. Their names were Moniek Kluger and Felek Zauberman. We all wound up in the U.S. near New York City. Our wives also became fast friends and our children grew up together.

38   LIFE AS A DISPLACED PERSON

The four of us had no problems getting into the camp with our official passes. We did as we were told and returned separately at different times, and the guards opened the gate and let us pass through with no questions. We were relieved to be inside where we could clean up, get some food and find a place to sleep for a bit.

The camp was Spartan and had few comforts but we felt safe and glad to be out of the elements. Lolek and I looked for a place where we could sleep. We went into one building and saw very quickly that every one of the beds was occupied. We went to some other buildings and in all of them the beds were taken. Finally, we came to another building and looked around. Again, the beds seemed to be all spoken for and we began to think we were going to have to sleep on the floor. But suddenly we caught the eyes of two very beautiful young girls who were sitting on the edge of one of the bunks. We went over to talk to them, telling them a little bit of our story—and they listened sympathetically. Then, to our surprise, the girls said to us, "Why don't the two of you take the top bunk and we will double up here on the bottom one?" We were floored by their sudden generosity and, not surprisingly, delighted that we could be in close company of these two lovely young women. So, we didn't hesitate to accept the offer and we quickly settled in.

I soon learned the names of our gracious hosts, but one of them had particularly caught my eye. Her name was Halina Goldberg. I was very attracted to her so I found any excuse to talk to her and get to know her better. Her friend's name was Lilka Silbiger and was also very friendly. But I was most interested in Halina and she seemed to return the interest in me that I had for her. At the time I was seventeen and she was sixteen. We would soon begin to spend a lot of time together. It didn't take her long to tell me her story.

Halina was from western Poland, in the town of Częstochowa, which, at the beginning of the war, was right on the border of Germany. She was on one of the infamous 'death marches' that the Nazis forced upon prisoners of their concentration and labor camps at the end of the war. As the Soviets advanced across Poland and the Allies approached from the west, the Germans began to evacuate prisoners from these camps in an attempt to hide the atrocities committed in them. Halina had miraculously survived one of the most notorious of these marches. In 1987, she did an oral testimony about her experience during the war. She was interviewed by the Holocaust Resource Center at Kean University in New Jersey. The interview was videotaped and is available online for viewing. It is a harrowing story with a miraculous ending and well worth the time it takes to view.

Austria had more than its fair share of displaced persons, as many of the other European countries were resisting accepting them. As a result, it wasn't always easy to get passes to leave the camp because the authorities there wanted to limit any potential problems and complaints from the locals about being overrun with refugees. But eager to explore in our newfound friendship, Halina and I found ways to sneak out. There was a place in the fence on the opposite side from the gate of the camp, hidden from constant watch by the guards, that could be lifted it up so we could scoot through to the outside. For me, it was great to have the freedom to slip away with Halina and go into town for a 'date.' It wasn't long before we were in somewhat of a courtship. We loved going into Salzburg to enjoy the parks and plazas. It was a city filled with music everywhere and there was a renewed optimism budding after the dark days of war. It was a romantic time for us. We went for picnics in the parks and we especially enjoyed going to a beautiful castle that stood on a nearby hilltop.

By coincidence, one of my friends from Tluste was at the DP camp in Salzburg. It was Wilo Schechner, the friend who demanded that his father hide me in their bunker during one of the early akcia. We were so happy to see each other again, and had soon related our stories of survival to each other. He told me that he was looking for a chance to get to Palestine, so we began to make a plan about how best we might do it.

The Americans controlled Salzburg at this time, and it was the center of their operations in Austria. There were several DP camps there, all of which were under the direction of the UNRRA, or the United Nations Relief and Rehabilitation Administration. Established toward the end of 1943. The organization provided aid to the war-torn areas of Europe. It was a forerunner of the United Nations, which was established later in 1945. We quickly learned there were several organizations helping Jews to get to Palestine, which had been under the authority of the British government since the end of World War I. But they had severely limited Jewish immigration to the region for many years and, immediately after the war they virtually stopped allowing it altogether. So, the organizations arranging for Jews to get into Palestine were doing so illegally. Undaunted by this, my friend and I decided we would take our chances and go there. We got in touch with an organization known as *Bricha* that was smuggling Jews through Southern Europe into Palestine and made our plans to go.

Because going there was prohibited, it wasn't an easy task to get to Palestine from Europe at that time. Those who were attempting it from Austria had to endure an arduous journey across the Alps on foot, get across the Italian border in some remote spot and then make their way to one of the port cities of Italy to catch a boat across the often-stormy Mediterranean. Our plan was to go to Innsbruck where we would meet the people who would help us get across the mountains to Italy. My heart was heavy at the thought of leaving Halina, but we were still very young and we did not yet have any thoughts of marriage. I still thought the best path for me was to join the thousands of other Jews who were eager to return to our forefather's homeland. So, we said our goodbyes and hoped to see each other again sometime in the near future.

In a few days Wilo and I were on our way to Innsbruck. Soon after we got there, we settled in with our hosts who would smuggle us to Italy. But not long after arriving, I suddenly began to feel very ill. I wasn't sure what the problem was, but I was finding it very difficult to breathe. I became more tired and weak with each passing hour. My back and shoulders ached and I was developing a persistent cough. At times I felt feverish. I began to wonder how I could make the grueling trek across the mountains, thousands of feet above sea level and through icy temperatures and snow in my current condition.

The next morning when it came time for us to leave, I told my friend that I didn't think I could make the journey because of my illness. I decided that I should return to the DP camp and rejoin Halina. The conflict of emotions that I felt at that time was overpowering. After my long ordeal, I yearned for a new life in a place where Jews would be accepted and safe from those who hated us. Now it seemed that dream was no longer possible. My heart sank. But the thought of seeing Halina again was a bright silver lining on the cloud of disappointment. I set out to get back to her as quickly as I could.

39 FACING DEATH ONE LAST TIME

I made my way back to Salzburg from Innsbruck only to learn that Halina had left there and was now at another camp nearby. The camp in Salzburg was crowded and uncomfortable. Like most of the DP camps, it offered poor conditions for the refugees. There were some efforts to try and improve them but resources were limited due to the vast number of other post-war priorities. Halina had learned that they were opening a new DP camp just a few miles east of Salzburg near a beautiful lakeside village named Ebensee. The camp was called Steinkogle and Halina had decided to go, hoping that the living arrangements would be better. When I found out she had gone there I decided to go there too. It was delightful to see her again and I arrived to find that this camp was much nicer than the one in Salzburg.

Once in Ebensee, my condition began to worsen. The pain in my chest and back was excruciating and I had developed a very bad cough. I could hardly sleep at night, as it was difficult to find a comfortable position with all the pain. I still didn't know what the illness was, but I knew I needed to get medical attention. At the camp there were two Jewish doctors. I went to them and they discovered that my lungs were filled with fluid. The diagnosis was pleurisy and I needed much more urgent care. So, they sent me immediately to Ebensee where there was as a makeshift hospital. I had not been in many hospitals in my life but I was surprised at how crude the facilities were. The beds were bunk beds and didn't have proper bedding, only crudely made mattresses stuffed with straw. There wasn't enough funding to keep them supplied with all the medications they needed. The conditions made me wonder how many people had survived all the horror of the Nazi murderers only to come to a facility like this and die because of the lack of proper medical treatment.

This facility had survivors from a concentration camp that had been near Ebensee. Many of these patients had contracted tuberculosis and were quarantined. Because of the long time they had all been there, they had formed a unique bond with one another. I would soon find myself a part of their tight knit group.

After I got settled into the hospital the doctors told me that it was imperative for me to have the fluid drained from my lungs as soon as possible. The procedure was generally done with a needle and syringe that was inserted between the ribs into the lungs and used to draw out the fluid. When it came time to do it, I learned that they had no anesthesia, and I would have to endure the painful injections without any painkillers. There were no private rooms that could be used to isolate me, so they conducted the procedure right in the bunkroom where the other patients also slept. A chair was placed in the middle of the room and I was asked to sit in it facing backwards so that my back was exposed toward the medics. As they prepared the syringe, I wrapped my arms around the back of the chair and held on tightly. I lowered my head, closed my eyes and waited. I felt a twinge of embarrassment since this was happening right in front of the other patients in the room.

I don't remember much detail about the pain I felt or how the procedure was carried out, but there was one thing that is etched in my memory. I can still hear the stream of fluid as it squirted from the syringe into the bottom of the bucket and splattered inside it. Time after time, the sound of the fluid being drained into the bucket pierced the silence in the room. It was a rhythmic progression that I hoped would end soon.

I was almost completely confined to bed for the following days. Halina had been coming to see me as often as she could, and the other patients and the doctors loved her visits nearly as much as I did. She had a lively personality and always put everyone at ease and in a good mood with her jovial disposition. She usually brought some treats to eat, cakes or cookies or something more savory but equally delicious. The comfort she brought me was no doubt a major factor in my eventual recovery. It seemed like a miracle to me that she could find such wonderful gifts to bring each time. But I was learning about her resourcefulness. She had made friends with some of the boys from the DP camp who were recruited to work in the kitchen of a nearby American Army base. With her charisma and charm, she convinced them to slip her some of the food they were preparing for the soldiers at the base.

During those first few days after my lungs had been drained, I wasn't showing much improvement. This would present another opportunity for Halina to show her resourcefulness. One day, Halina came to visit again and one of the doctors pulled her aside and said, "Lonek is in danger of becoming very sick. He needs some medicine, which we don't have here. If he doesn't get it, he will develop tuberculosis and he may die." With a worried look Halina asked, "What is it and where can I get it?" The doctor told her it was a medicine made from calcium and that she could try to find it at one of the other DP camps. Halina left immediately to find the drug. She went back to the camp in Salzburg to see if they might have it there. When she arrived, she ran into one of our friends, Salci Perecman, a Lithuanian Jew who had a very big and imposing figure. Older than we were, Salci was a rough and tough-looking character. When she explained why she was there, he said, "Let's go into town and see if we can find it at the local pharmacy."

The two of them arrived at the pharmacy and approached the pharmacist, asking whether he had the calcium in stock. When he said he didn't, Halina pleaded with the man, explaining that my life was in danger if she couldn't get the drugs. The man insisted again that he didn't have the medication. At that point, Salci stepped up to the counter and pulled himself to full height. He peered into the man's eyes intently then said in a stern voice, "We need this medication." The man once again denied that he had it. Then Salci slowly reached into his pocket and pulled out a pocketknife. He raised the knife slightly and then plunged it down hard, sticking it into the wooden countertop. Then he said to the pharmacist, "I'm not sure you understood me. We need this medication now." Nervously the man said, "I understand. I'll get it for you." He turned quickly, found the bottles containing the drug and prepared the dosage as fast as he could. Salci and Halina took it, thanked the man and hurried back to the hospital. The medication played a crucial part in getting me back to health. The threat of contracting TB had been minimized and the doctors no longer worried about that. But it wasn't an overnight process, and I had to remain in the hospital for many weeks before making a full recovery.

I had been there about a month when we were told all the patients were to be transferred to hospitals with proper facilities and staff. None of us liked the thought of moving and resettling into an unfamiliar facility, despite our poor health conditions. Most of the men in my ward were afflicted with tuberculosis. So far, I had escaped the disease but the pleurisy had left me tired and weakened as much as any of the others.

All of us complained to one another about the possible move and some of the patients determined that they wouldn't go. They had simply set their minds to resist and stay put. The idea gained traction and soon almost every one of us agreed that we would fight the move. The doctors learned of this and tried to reassure us that these hospitals would be much better prepared to care for us. But they were not successful in convincing us. The cry that resounded across the room was, "We don't know where they're taking us. We're not moving! We're not moving!"

It's seems illogical that men in such a weakened condition would react this way. But one has to understand that what we had endured under the Nazis over the last five years of our lives had made us overly suspicious of any authority, friend or foe. The hospital at Ebensee was crude and makeshift and it didn't even have nurses to care for us. But our common experiences surviving the Holocaust and now fighting lung disease had formed a very strong bond between us all. We could not bear the thought of being separated. We enjoyed the stability and comfort of being in a familiar place and became afraid of the unknown that a move would bring.

When the day came for us to be transported out, we decided to resist. We bound ourselves all together with ropes to make it difficult to remove us from our beds. Seeing our plan, the doctors called for the military police to come and forcibly remove us. One by one the MP's cut our ropes and put us all into awaiting ambulances for the trip.

I was sent to a hospital a little higher up in the mountains in a town called Goisern, just a few miles south of Ebensee. When I arrived there, I felt a bit silly for being a part of such a protest. This hospital was a beautiful place, fully staffed with nuns who were professional nurses. The doctors seemed more proficient and the rooms were much more private and the beds were the most comfortable beds I had slept in for many years. The pillows and bedding were plush and clean. The food was delicious and we had everything we needed medically to make a swift recovery. The mountain air there was also very invigorating—just what my lungs needed—and the nurses took me for walks every day to take it in. I was so glad our little plan of resistance had failed. Now I was well on my way to getting back to full health.

A few more weeks passed and I was finally cured and ready to leave the hospital. Halina had returned to Salzburg so I made my way back there. It was so good to see her again and we decided we would live together there. In the meantime, however, my friend Lolek had decided to return to Krakow. When he got there. he found my sister and told her that I had been ill. Tusia immediately took a train to Salzburg to see how her little brother was doing. When she arrived, she was very relieved to see that I had fully recovered.

Tusia told us that she had heard there were some friends of ours from Tarnopol living in the town of Schwandorf, Germany. We decided that we would go there for a while to see them and perhaps settle there if we found it desirable. So, we packed up and, within a few days, we left for there. Mendel joined us and not long after Edek came as well. Edek had moved to the town of Breslau, which is now known as Wroclaw, after I left Krakow. There he met his future wife, Ina Bergman, and they were married there.

Not long after we arrived in Schwandorf, Halina was given an opportunity to move to America. Since she was younger than 18 and had no family left to support her so she was put high atop the priority list of refugees for immigrating. I was happy for her of course, but saddened that we would soon be separated. The process moved quickly and soon she was ready to leave. We said our goodbyes and wished each other well. We both had high hopes that we would see each other again.

Of course, I had thought often about immigrating to America. But at the time, immigration was being limited and one had to have a relative there to make sure they would be taken care of financially and otherwise. These relatives had to promise that the immigrants wouldn't take a job that could go to a U.S. citizen and would have to support them financially if they couldn't do so themselves. My aunt was there and she had been in favor of all of us coming to live there. But it was a lot to ask of her, so for the time being, I put the thought aside.

I don't remember how long I stayed in Schwandorf with my brother and sister. But soon I grew tired of living in the small apartment with the rest of my family. I was eager to get out and find my own way. So, I decided to get back into school and was admitted to a gymnasium in the nearby town of Regensburg. In Germany, a gymnasium is the highest level of schooling before university or college. By total coincidence, my friend Sam visited the town and we happened to meet at a local center where Jews would gather socially. Once again, our paths had crossed and our friendship deepened.

In Regensburg, I rented a room with a family that was very stereotypically German. They were provincial in their outlook and lived a very simple life. Our relationship was strained, as they did not want to interact with me very much and vice versa. I don't know why but they seemed to view me with some suspicion. As I came to and went from the house on my daily activities, I tried my best to avoid them. Whenever we did see each other we exchanged normal pleasantries but we never carried the conversation any further than that. They had a daughter who was near my age but probably a couple of years younger. I was not interested in her romantically but I was to find out rudely one night that she was in me. I stumbled out of bed in the middle of that night to go to the bathroom. When I opened the door, I was shocked to find her in the bath. She motioned for me to come in and then she reached for me. I quickly retreated slamming the door and ran back to my bed. I knew then and there that I could not stay with them any longer. The very next day I made plans to return to Schwandorf.

In the meantime, my aunt in America had been searching for us. We had not been diligent in keeping her informed of the various moves we had made in the past few years so she had no way to contact us. But she was persistent and kept up the search. Fortunately, she had a son-in-law who was a doctor and an officer serving in the army in Germany at the time. She tasked him with tracking us down and eventually he did through the UNRAA organization. He came to visit us in Schwandorf and announced that our aunt wanted to help us immigrate to the U.S. We were all thrilled at the news and we began to prepare for it. There was a lot of paperwork and correspondence to take care of so it took a few months to accomplish. Edek and Ina were the first to be accepted and they left in August of 1946. I would be next, but it would take another year to complete the process. Tusia, Mendel and Fryma came two months after me.

In October of 1947, I stepped on board the S.S. Ernie Pyle, a well-remembered ship that transported new immigrants to the United States after the war. A couple of months earlier I had turned 19. Even though that time was only a small part of my life, those eight long years from the start of the war would shape and define me.

My long voyage to America had begun. Once again, I felt great conflicting emotions. The promise of America with all its prosperity filled me with excitement for what seemed to be an array of hopeful possibilities. I had seen the images of its people living the good life with every luxury available to them. But on the other hand, I knew about the struggles of immigrants who had arrived with little or nothing, and struggled just to get by. Many of them worked their hands to the bone in sweatshops and factories. I hardly knew any English, I hadn't had any schooling since the war had started, and I had no professional skills. That reality beset me with fear and trepidation.

As the ship sailed on, it rose and sank as it ploughed through the waves. So did my spirits contemplating the future in a very strange land. But I had risen to the challenge of survival in the midst of unimaginable evil, and fortune had smiled on my will to live. I knew I would find the courage to face whatever challenges might still lie ahead.

AFTERWORD

My arrival in America wasn't the end of my trials and tribulations. Considering what I had been through during the Nazi reign of terror, the difficulties I faced were considerably much easier to bear. I would never want to repeat that horrible nightmare, but there is no question that going through it imbued me with a strength to endure during difficult times.

I was now in the land of opportunity, but no one was ready to hand success to me on a platter. No one I encountered in the United States wanted to hear my story. I was not surprised and neither did I expect anyone to give me any special favor because of my ordeal. I had learned well through it all that the only way to survive is through hard work, diligence and persistence.

That is not to say that my survival was all due to my own efforts. It is estimated that 90 percent of the Jews in Poland died during the Holocaust. We had great help from our unlikely hero, Timush along the way who did what he could to assist us. As my story documents—and also the stories of so many others—there was a lot of improbable luck that came our way allowing us to escape. But without the strong will to survive and the fortitude to do whatever it takes, no goal can be achieved, no matter how large or small it may be. In the end, it was that drive to live that made the difference.

It was difficult trying to find work. My English was not very good and I had very little education and no skills. So, I went through several attempts and disappointments applying for jobs. In the meantime, my friend Lolek had made his way to New York. He had family living in Queens, so we were able to reconnect. When I went to visit them early on in my job search, they counseled me, "Lonek isn't an English name. You need to change it if you want to get a job." So, they began to toss out suggestions that began with my first initial. After they had floated several ideas, such as Leonard, Lenny, Larry—I thought of a boyhood nickname I had used before the war. "How about Leon?" I asked. It was a common English name, so they agreed it would work. Later on, in life, I was sorry that I hadn't kept Lonek as my name. I never understood why they thought it was a problem. It wasn't the only unusual name you heard on the streets of New York, even in those days.

Nevertheless, once my name was changed, Lolek's family helped me get a job on the lower East Side of Manhattan at a fabric store in the clothing industry. The business, known as Beckenstein, is still operating today. While I worked there, I was considered what is known in Polish as a *przynieś, wynieś, pozamiataj*. It means someone who "brings in, takes out and sweeps." In other words, it was someone who does all the little undesirable tasks. In English slang you would call such a person a 'gopher.' Some who "goes for this, and goes for that." But the Polish phrase rhymes and is much more colorful in my opinion.

My aunt and uncle had been very generous to me allowing me to live with them, feeding me and providing many of the basic things I needed. Now that I had a job, I could give back a little bit for my room and board.

All was good in the arrangement until they began to suspect I was interested in their daughter romantically. Her name was Gloria and she was my cousin. But she was so beautiful I couldn't help but flirt with her. She wasn't shy about returning the affection. Our banter didn't go unnoticed by my live-in relatives. Then one day, the flirting turned into a little bit more than just enticing words. We were in the lobby of the apartment building and suddenly we began to kiss. As luck would have it, the elevator opened and my aunt and uncle were staring right at us. Understandably, that was the last straw for them and they told me I would have to leave and find another place to live.

As I thought about where I could go, I remembered Halina was now in Buffalo. I missed her and decided to go visit her. Halina was able to find me a place to stay with a friend of hers named Gerda Klein. Gerda had been in the death camp and the death march with Halina. She became a human rights activist as a result of her ordeal and a well-known writer and speaker about the Holocaust. Her story was made into a short film that won both an Oscar and an Emmy.

Halina accomplished something truly remarkable during her time in Buffalo, which I am very proud of her to this day. Because of the war, she had never been to high school, but now she had the opportunity to make up for that lost time. And did she ever! She enrolled in a local high school bound and determined to get her diploma. Even though she was seventeen and older than most of the other students, she would have to start from the beginning as a freshman. This did not discourage her in the least and, in fact, it gave her the determination to work extremely hard to finish school as fast as possible. This would not be an easy task, especially considering that she had almost no knowledge of English when she started. With Polish-to-English dictionaries in her hands at all times, she toiled through the classes, not only forced to learn the course work, but to learn English at the same time. Despite these great obstacles, she completed the four-year high school degree in only two years! I was so happy to escort her to her high school prom and then to attend her graduation to celebrate her momentous achievement.

Not only did Gerda Klein and her husband, Kurt, allow me to live with them, but he was also able to get me a job as a shipping clerk in a local sporting goods shop. I stayed for about six months until I heard from Edek that he needed help in his newly purchased grocery store in Brooklyn. My aunt had given him a loan to buy the shop and he was determined to be successful in this new business. So, I decided to leave and go help him.

Eventually the business struggled and we sold it. From then on, I tried my hand at several ventures. I worked in a large textile shop in Manhattan for a while, then as an insurance salesman, and after that as a merchandiser for a company supplying all kinds of products to grocery store chains. I did all right at all these jobs but I really wanted to work for myself and become an independent businessman. That was my dream and the goal I set to accomplish. So, when the opportunity came to me to take over an independent business peddling merchandise door-to-door around Brooklyn, I jumped at it. The service had a good base of clients already buying the products on a regular basis. The products were all household products that the customers needed on a regular basis, so it was a source of good cash flow right from the start.

I was doing well with the peddling business but it was becoming a dangerous job. The neighborhoods in my territory were not the safest. Criminals knew salesmen like me carried a lot of money since door-to-door transactions in those days were always in cash. The reports of assaults on other peddlers began to increase. And then, after a few close calls with some potential robbers, I decided it was time for a change.

In the meantime, Edek had invested in a real estate partnership in New Jersey that was building new apartments and homes. Following the war there was a growing demand for new homes as the population, along with the American economy, was booming. The members of the partnership were looking for additional partners to continue to expand and keep up with the demand.

I took all that I had saved up and decided to join them. I knew nothing about construction or real estate, but they told me, "Don't worry. We'll teach you everything you need to know." I was a diligent student and I worked hard to learn everything I could about every aspect of the business. I wasn't content with being a passive investor and only an executive sitting in the company office. I spent hours on the job sites, watching and learning from the skilled tradesmen—engineers, architects, surveyors, carpenters and plumbers—until eventually I knew the business from every angle. The business grew steadily through the years as we became ever more skilled in the real estate and construction industries.

Halina and I were married on October 24, 1949. We were blessed with a beautiful and loving family, two daughters and a son. Our family life has been one of great joy but also great heartache. My oldest daughter, Susan, was born in 1952 and she lives near me in New Jersey. She has three daughters, Jamie, Danielle and Carly. Jamie and Danielle are married now and starting their own families. Jamie's husband's name is Gilad and Danielle's wife's is Maryann. To our great delight, Jamie gave birth to our first great grandson early in 2018. His name is Liev Max Jacobs. Carly is now living in Washington, D.C. and working as a marketing coordinator for the National Geographic Channel.

My youngest daughter, Nina, was born in 1967. She has two beautiful children with some very creative names. Her boy is named Xander and her daughter is named Drew. We don't get to see her as often as we wished since she and her husband, Noah, now live in Los Angeles.

My son David was born a little over a year after Susan and was very bright and intelligent. We loved him greatly and he brought great joy to us. He was doing extremely well as a communications major at Boston University when he was diagnosed with brain cancer. His brave fight against the dreaded disease was inspirational. But sadly, after two years of chemotherapy, surgery and various treatments, he passed away. It was two years of hell and agony for all of us. We miss him greatly but remember him fondly and lovingly every day.

Looking back on all that I experienced I would have to say that, in the end, I had a wonderful life. But it was one of great extremes and I have seen both the best life can offer and the absolute worse. My very early years in Tarnopol were pleasant and joyful. They were quickly followed by a few years of unimaginable horror as the Germans wreaked havoc on all of Eastern Europe. That span was only five years, a small percentage of my total, but they loom large and were the defining part of my life in many ways. I was lucky to survive and make my way to the United States where the best part of life began for me.

The purpose of this book is to establish a record of the evil my family suffered and to give credit to the man who sacrificed all to help us survive. If there can be a silver lining to the horror of the Holocaust, stories like mine, and those of the many other Eastern European Jews who survived and eventually thrived, are bright edges of that very dark cloud. There is no doubt that the sufferings we endured gave us exceptional strength to face anything that we encountered later in life. I know that my terrible experiences during the war helped me endure the death of my son David. I had learned that life is not always fair and that one must accept what fate delivers in order to overcome adversity.

However, it is very difficult for me to accept the idea that there was anything positive that came from the Holocaust. Yes, I miraculously survived and was able to lead a full and abundant life beyond my wildest imaginings as young boy in Tarnopol. But the reality that six million others were brutally murdered and denied any chance for a wonderful life like mine will always be the lens through which I view the happy ending to my story. We can never allow such a tragedy to occur again. My hope is that my story can stand with all the others to help prevent history from repeating itself.

HOW WE LEARNED OF TIMUSH AND HANIA'S FATE

For years after the war we yearned to know what had happened to Timush and Hania. Then in 1985, as the Soviet Union began to open up under *Perestroika*, I decided to visit Tluste and find our parents' graves. Even under *Perestroika* it was not easy to arrange travel behind the Iron Curtain. But we were eager and determined so we made the effort. During those times you still had to have an official escort wherever you went in the Soviet Union. It was sometime in the spring of 1985 that we left for Moscow. Halina, my daughter Susan and her former husband went too. It was a strange feeling to be there, constantly under the watchful eyes of our escorts. We were certain we were being examined at all times and all our communication monitored.

After a few days in Moscow, we traveled to Tarnopol where we would stay for the entire visit to the area since there really was not suitable lodging in Tluste at the time. The hotel in Tarnopol was very Spartan and quite below Western standards. But we would not be here long and we were not here for the sheer pleasure of touring.

Sometime before our visit, Edek and Tusia visited Tarnopol and by sheer coincidence they met one of my friends from long ago in Tluste. My friend's name was Zysio Stup and he had left Tluste with the Soviets when the Germans first invaded. He was Jewish and, like many Eastern European Jews, he joined the Red Army and fought with them through the entire war. Fortunately, he survived and after the war he settled in Tarnopol. He was a school friend of mine in those days and Edek and Tusia had never known him. So how they found him is an interesting story.

When Edek and Tusia made their trip, Tusia's sons, Steven and Jerry, and Steven's wife, Nancy, went with them. On their first night there, they ate in the restaurant of the hotel in which they were staying. A band was playing for the patrons dining there. When the band took a break from playing, the leader started to walk toward them. He introduced himself and then asked who they were and where were they from. They explained they were visiting from America and here to see where they had grown up. The band member, then turned toward Steven and asked, "Are you by chance Mendel Weinstock's son?" They were all taken aback and wondered how the man knew this. The man was Zysio and he explained that when he first saw Steven, he looked so much like Mendel that he must be a relative. He had known Mendel very well even though he did not know Edek or Tusia. This twist of fate allowed me to reconnect with him and eventually to find out more of the story of what happened to Timush and Hania. When the band struck up again, Zysio played a special song for all of them. It was the beautiful Jewish folk song, 'Jerusalem of Gold.'

When I began to make my plans to go to Tluste, I decided that I would try to visit Zysio. I was eager to see him again after so many years but I also reasoned that he could give me help with or advice about getting to Tluste. But because of the tight control of the Soviets it was impossible to contact him before arriving there. Since Edek and Tusia had found him on their trip, I was hopeful that I would be able to find him also. So, once there we made our way to the restaurant and luckily, he was still working there. He was an accomplished musician and was still playing music there with his band. We were very happy to see each other and spent some time reminiscing and telling our stories of survival. Then he told us that he would like to have us to his home for a meal one evening while we were in town. But under the Soviets, he would have to get special permission from the authorities to host us. It took several days, but eventually our request was granted. It was a delightful meal, a joyful evening and so good to reconnect with him.

The next day we traveled to Tluste together with our Soviet escort. Tluste is only about 100 kilometers from Tarnopol but it was not easy getting there. The train service was not dependable or adequate so we hired a driver to take us there by car. The roads were very rough and were not made for fast travel. What should have taken us a few hours took us almost a half a day.

Once there we made our way to the place where the executions had occurred on Black Thursday. The place of this mass grave is still known and is the final resting place of my mother, grandmother and aunt who were murdered there along with more than 3,000 other Jews from Tluste. Gazing over the site brought back the terrible memories of that day and the grief I felt for my mother's awful fate. We stood in silence for several minutes to honor those who lost their lives here.

In a little while, as we stood by the graves, an old lady who had been watching us with great curiosity from nearby began to approach. She was a small woman, a bit portly and slightly hunched over from years of hard work. She wore a babushka on her head and she looked like the stereotypical peasant woman from Eastern Europe. She said hello to us in Ukrainian and asked us who we were and why we were there. Our guide explained why we had come and suddenly she straightened up with great interest. I could understand their conversation completely of course, so I translated for the rest of my family.

She began to tell us that she was a little girl living in Tluste when the events of my story had taken place. And then, to our great surprise, she began to recount the terrible events of Black Thursday. She had been there, right at the spot where the executions had taken place over the pit. She described every detail exactly as we had heard it from the other survivors and witnesses. Her account confirmed the huge pit that had been dug, the plank laid across it and the machine gun deployed to shoot the victims. She told us how the Jews were forced to undress completely and fold their clothes and place them on the back of the trucks assembled there.

Then she told us about the days after the massacre and how the grave heaved and groaned. She remembered the awful stench and the eerie mist that rose above the cemetery. With a voice that clearly revealed the day had a frightening effect on her, she said that the locals all thought these phenomena were signs that the god of the Jews was showing his great displeasure at what had occurred there.

I continued to translate it all for my family but the emotions welled up inside of me as I thought of my dear mother and her terrible fate. How I longed to know what those last moments had been like for her. I longed to know her final thoughts and imagined how awful the pain and anguish must have been. Then I thought of what Timush had told us as he saw her being marched toward the execution site. And suddenly I knew at least a little bit of the answer. Her last thoughts were on us, her children, as she cried to him, "Please, save my children."

From that thought came the name of this book. So many mothers and fathers lost their children to an inexplicable cruelty and hatred. So many children lost their parents. So many had their lives stolen from them primarily because of the madness of one man. But others were complicit. There was also a ready willingness to believe and follow that incarnation of evil itself. How almost an entire nation, one my father thought was the most cultured in the history of humanity, could fall prey to the deception, hatred and violence is beyond understanding.

After we left the mass grave, we made our way to the Jewish cemetery where my father was buried. When we arrived we found it to be totally neglected. Cows and goats grazed on the overgrown weeds and grass that had engulfed it. Many of the headstones were broken and vandalized and many others were completely knocked over.

We searched hard to find my father's grave but it was impossible to locate. We had not been able to put a proper headstone on it and any trace of where the grave had been dug was long gone. It was difficult for me to remember even the general area where he had been buried and any grave without a solid marker was completely unrecognizable. I was very disappointed to say the least.

In spite of not knowing exactly where he was, we had come prepared to say a prayer and we gathered together to do that. I recited a traditional Jewish Kaddish and we all kept a few moments of silence. I remembered as best I could all the things about my father—his hard work and his devotion to his family, his love of music and culture, how he and my mother danced to the music on the radio. So many memories came flooding back that soon I was overtaken by sadness and I wept.

Years later, after the Berlin Wall finally came down, we were able to visit Tarnopol and Tluste again. It was much easier by that time to get into the country and we did not need any special escort or guide. It was still a difficult place to travel and not a comfortable trip. On this trip we were hoping we could find and meet Timush and Hania's son, Lubko.

We did not know where he lived or even if he was still alive but we were eager to find out. This time I was able to contact Zysio beforehand and we asked him to help us find Lubko. Zysio was very happy to help and began the search. Surprisingly, he learned that Lubko lived only a few blocks away from him in Tarnopol. So, we contacted him and asked him if we could come visit him.

At first, he was very reluctant to agree to meet with us. Americans were still considered suspect and not well liked by many who had grown up in the Soviet system. But after we told him of his father and mother's heroics, he agreed to let us visit him. He also volunteered to take us to Tluste himself. So, we made our plans to return to Tarnopol and Tluste. This time we were able to take my daughter, Nina, and my granddaughter, Jamie.

The closest airport to Tarnopol is in Lwów. When we landed there, Lubko was waiting for us at the airport. He had come in an old worn out pickup truck that had seen much better days. He drove us the 128 kilometers to Tarnopol and welcomed us into his home. A rough ride to say the least, but we were so happy to have found him and finally be able to tell him the full story. We met his wife and family and had a lovely time getting to know each other.

Lubko was very surprised to learn about the sacrifice his parents had made for us. Since Timush and Hania had been very careful to keep the secret of the bunker from him, He had been totally unaware of those long-ago events. When Timush left to fight with the Germans, Lubko was still very young and knew nothing of our hiding in his parents' house. Of course, Timush never returned to tell him, and his mother died not too long after the war without ever having done so.

Lubko was very grateful to learn about the sacrifices made by both his parents and was moved by their valor. We made it our mission to help him and his family in every way that we could, including occasional financial support over the many years we knew him. Sadly, Lubko is no longer alive, but we continue to help his children, as we are able. In some small way, we have been able to return some compensation for what Timush and Hania did for us.

Timush and Hania both have memorials in Tluste for their service and sacrifice for an independent Ukraine. At those sites there is nothing about what they did to save our family. I had long thought that they should be recognized for taking such great risk and going to such great lengths to keep us alive. The proper place for that was not in Tluste but at the Yad Vashem Holocaust Memorial in Jerusalem. This place is very special and the designers, architects, builders and historians who made it a reality are to be highly congratulated.

One of the more important places in the museum is the section that is dedicated to 'righteous Gentiles.' These were the non-Jewish people who helped save Jews through great risk and heroics during the Nazi reign. Only those who did so for noble reasons and not for money or personal gain can be recognized at the memorial. There was no doubt that Timush and Hania deserved to be honored there. So, I became determined to make it happen. I contacted Yad Vashem and the curators began their very thorough process to verify our story. Once completed, they agreed that they should be honored there. On September 9, 1988 it became official and Tusia and I were able to attend the ceremony at Yad Vashem in Jerusalem.

Looking back now over those terrible years in which we faced hatred, starvation, disease, war and death all around us, it is now easier for me to process the emotions of it. While I worked with the writers and editors who helped me pen my story, they constantly asked me to describe how the events affected me emotionally at the moment they occurred. But my memory at most points of the story could not bring those feelings back. In fact, I think the events were just so overwhelming in the moment that I really did not feel much of anything there and then. I think that is the natural reaction for the mind when it is subjected to so much horror compressed over so little time. But primarily, it was a matter of survival. The only thing we could think about was how to live to the next day or moment. There was no time for emotions.

At this writing, antisemitism is once again on the rise throughout the world. In Eastern Europe, governments are coming to power that openly express suspicion and hatred for Jews. It is also happening in many other parts of the world such as Asia, Central and South America. And even in the United States we are not immune. There are more and more people joining Neo-Nazi organizations and other hate groups who are not beyond using violence to attack Jewish people. The freedom of the Internet has allowed them to spread their hate-filled propaganda much more quickly and easily. So, it is very naïve indeed to think that what happened under Adolf Hitler cannot happen again.

But I believe my story gives us some reason for optimism. Every story of the Holocaust must be remembered and continue to be told. They are each important and unique. I hope that I have been successful in conveying both of those qualities about my story and that each reader is edified by it. My brother and sister told their stories in the Shoah interviews. But those interviews were limited and neither gave the entire story of our family.

This is the first attempt to publish it fully. First and foremost, it is the story of my family. But my primary purpose for finally getting it on record is to pay tribute to our unlikely hero, Timush. His amazing transformation and bravery show that it is possible for hatred and violence can be overcome. Let's hope and pray that those who are consumed by those traits in today's world will also find a way to overcome them. It is the only way to prevent another Holocaust.

ACKNOWLEDGMENTS

Several outside sources were used to relate events that I did not personally witness. I would like to acknowledge those people and sources that helped me give a fuller picture of everything that was happening around me and affected my story.

I am extremely grateful to my brother, Edek, and my sister, Tusia, for having the fortitude to complete the interviews requested by Stephen Spielberg's Shoah Foundation. Their videotaped accounts helped me tremendously in putting together the accurate record of our story.

After their deaths, the realization that our story had never been fully told to a greater audience began to haunt me. Their willingness to sit through the hours required to do the interviews motivated me to find the courage and strength to fulfill the difficult task that writing a book requires.

Long before the Shoah interviews, my nephews and Tusia's sons, Steven and Jerry Weinstock interviewed all three of us in great detail. In the 1970s, with help from Edek's son, Stewart, they compiled a very descriptive account of the story focusing on the war years and up until our escape from the bunker. I am indebted to their hard work and attention to detail in getting much of the story fleshed out and documenting parts of which I was not very familiar. Thanks also to Steven for digitizing the sketch of the bunker done by Edek. He also replaced the original handwriting that labeled the sketch with more legible type.

I would like to thank Doug Hykle, whose family hails from our little town of Tluste. Doug is of Ukrainian descent and has been working tirelessly for many years to compile a detailed history of Tluste. His work to establish a timetable for events there during the war was very helpful. He has also done much to document the Jewish families that lived in Tluste before the war and where in the town each of them lived.

The diary by Dr. Baruch Milch, a physician living in Tluste and our family doctor, was an inspiration for me to finally tell my story. Dr. Milch began his account while in hiding and he scrounged for every scrap piece of paper he could find to make sure the evil occurring around him was documented. He completed the diary years after he moved to Tel Aviv, but it was not published until after his death. His daughters, Shosh Milch-Avigal and Ella Sheriff worked hard to make sure it was completed and published. His account, along with several others, of the Black Thursday massacre in Tluste was a primary source for my version. The book, *Can Heaven be Void*, was edited by Shosh Milch-Avigal and published by Yad Vashem in 2003. Sadly, Shosh died shortly before the book was published. Ella completed the process and now it is available from Yad Vashem in English.

Thanks to Dina Kleiner, Stewart Kleiner's daughter and my grand niece, for collecting and cataloging the photos that were taken before the war.

I am deeply indebted to my good friend Sam Langholz without whom I may not be here today to tell my story. We have been friends for almost 80 years and were young boys fighting for survival at the same time in Tluste. He was a constant inspiration to keep me focused and motivated to tell my story and finish the book. And without his help in reconstructing the events we faced together during those dark days, much would have been forgotten or inaccurate.

Last, but certainly not least, I want to thank my lovely wife, Halina. I could not have completed the retelling of my story without her love and support. The feedback she provided as we crafted the story was invaluable. And, as she has been throughout our lives together, she was a constant source of inspiration and encouragement.

PHOTOS

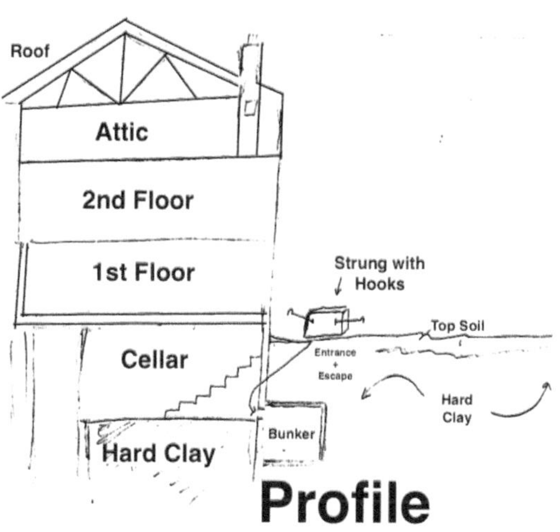

Bunker outside view, drawn by Edek

Timush and Hania (although of bad quality, it is worthwhile including in this book)

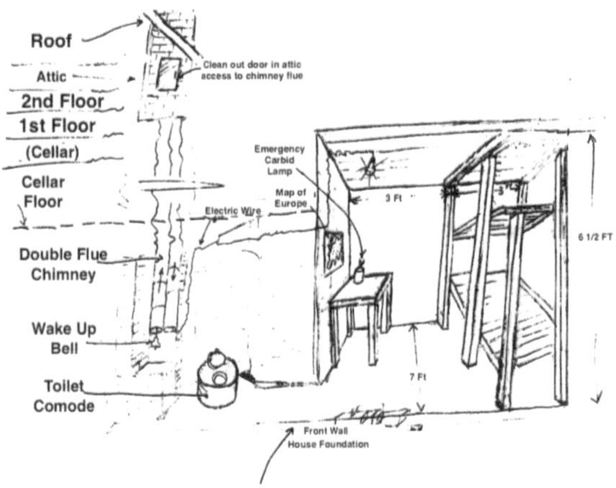

Bunker inside view, drawn by Edek

Leon's parents, shortly before the outbreak of WW2

Leon's grandparents from his father's side

Employees of the Kleiner Bickel hat factory.
Leon's father is seated on the left

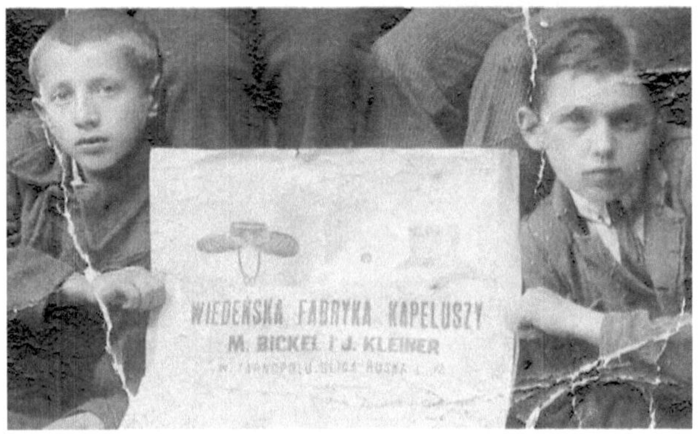

Boys holding a placard of the Kleiner Bickel hat
factory

Leon as a baby

Leon dressed as Ali Baba

Leon with top hat and cane

Leon on the town square in Tarnopol

Edek and Tusia on a tricycle

Edek and Tusia in costume

The Kleiner siblings and some friends. Leon is
wearing his white sailor hat

The Kleiner siblings

The Kleiner siblings on vacation. Leon is wearing
his white sailor hat

The Kleiner family at the beach

Leon's family with mother and Zosia, the nanny

The Kleiner family in Iwonich. Leon is dressed in a
white outfit

Leon in horse-drawn cart

Leon's father during summer in Tartarow. He is highlighted near the back

Leon highlighted on photo taken during festival of Purim

Leon highlighted during Chanukkah

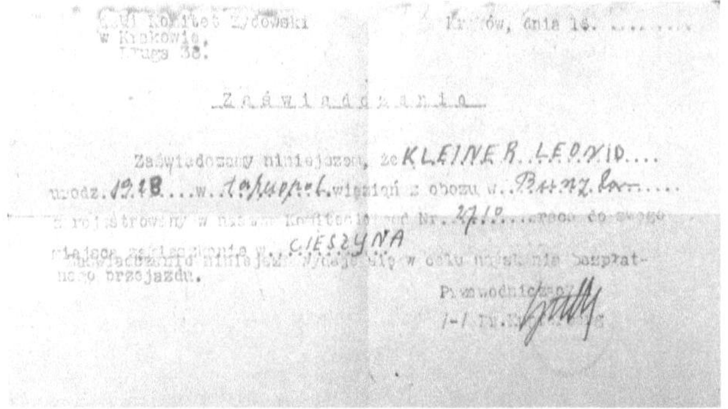

Leon's Krakow-Prague travel document, falsely
mentioning the Bunzlau concentration camp

Leon in Prague. Leon and behind him Lolek are highlighted

Leon in German alleyway, probably Schwandorf

EMIGRATION AND REPATRIATION
ASSEMBLY & PROCESSING CENTER
Called from Consulate
C L E A R A N C E   S L I P
W e g w e i s e r   A7DC

TO: KLEINER LEON   REGISTRATION NO: 10,222
Für: ....   Registrier No: ....

Go to the following rooms in the order indicated:
Gehen Sie zu den folgenden Stellen/Zimmern, melden
Sie sich der Reihe nach:

		INITIALS
		DEPARTURE
1. REGISTRATION	30 IX 47	
2. MEDICAL & DESINFECTION / Doktor und Desinfektion		
3. BILLETING / Wohnungsanweisung		
4. GO TO BLOCK / Gehen Sie zum Block		
5. BLOCK LEADER / Block-Leiter Block		

If you have any questions your Blockleader or the persons in information office will answer them.
Wenn Sie irgendwelche Fragen haben, werden Ihr Block-
leiter oder die Angestellten vom Informationsbüro
dies zu beantworten versuchen.

READ THE BULLETIN BOARD DAILY
LESEN SIE DIE .... TÄGLICH

Visa issued on Sept 25. 47

Leon's immigration document, dated 25 September
1947

Leon and his siblings after the war near lake
Schwandorf. On the ground on the left is Aunt
Fryma and Edek's wife, Ina, is on the right.

U.S.S. Ernie Pyle, one of the ships that brought
refugees and immigrants to America after the war

Leon on the U.S.S. Ernie Pyle

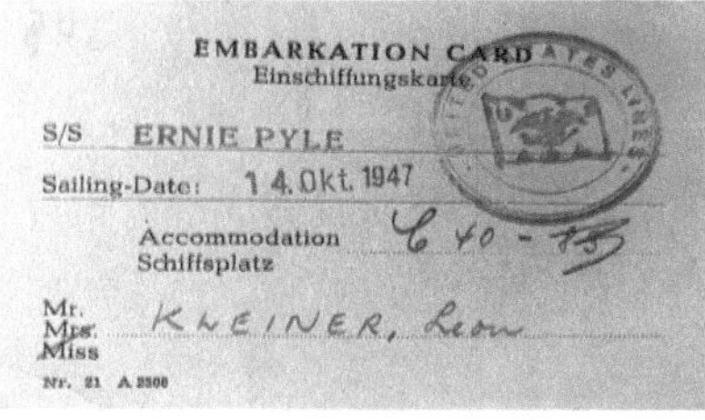

Leon's embarkation card

Leon's 'Alien registration card

Leon and Lubko and families in the Ukraine (2005)

Leon and Lubko

Leon and Lubko's wife

Lubko's family in Tluste

Kleiners at Yad Vashem in Jeruzalem (2012)

David Kleiner during his fight with cancer

Leon and Halina soon after marriage in 1949

Leon's 90th birthday celebration in the summer of
2018

Popi Kleiner tapestry which miraculously survived
the war

Kleiner Holocaust memorial plaque at Temple
Beth Ahm Yisrael in Springfield, NJ

Kleiner Holocaust memorial plaque at Temple
Beth Ahm Yisrael in Springfield, NJ

Leon Kleiner is a retired commercial and residential real estate developer from New Jersey. He was born in the city of Tarnopol, Poland just a little over a decade before the beginning World War II. After the war, the city became a part of the Ukraine and still is today. Leon's early life before and during the war is documented in this book. He miraculously survived the Holocaust and immigrated to America in 1947 where he married his wife, Halina, who is also a survivor of the Holocaust. They met in a displaced persons camp in Austria in 1945. He and his brother worked hard to save up enough money to invest in a real estate company that was benefiting from the post-war housing boom. In 1964, he moved from New York to New Jersey where he formed a new real estate company with his brother. Their business grew and prospered over the following years. Now in his nineties, he is enjoying retirement with Halina, who also wrote her Holocaust story: *My March Through Hell. A Young Girls's Terrifying Journey to Survival* (Amsterdam Publishers, 2022). They are the proud parents of two daughters. They also had a son who was tragically lost to cancer in his early twenties. His daughters have given them five grandchildren and they just recently welcomed their first great grandson.

Edwin Stepp has more than 30 years experience in media, marketing and advertising. He was executive editor for the quarterly, *Vision. Journal for a New World*, for over 15 years. The magazine had a modest circulation but was distributed in over 75 countries worldwide. He wrote dozens of articles about history, culture, environment and current events for the publication. The magazine had a companion Website that had over 250,000 visitors per month. Edwin lead the development of the Website and also a mobile app for additional distribution of the content. In that position he also helped write and edit several books about Jewish and Christian history published by the journal. In 2011, Edwin founded Django Productions, a television and film production company that focuses on documentaries and nonfiction entertainment. Edwin continues to hone his writing talents as he develops these films and their scripts.

Thank you very much for reading this memoir. We hope you enjoyed reading it and would love to ask you to post a few kind words on Amazon or on Goodreads. Alternatively, if you have read this as Kindle eBook, you could simply leave a rating. That is just one click, indicating how many stars of five you think this book deserves. This will only cost you a split second.

Many thanks in advance!

Leon Kleiner and Edwin Stepp

Holocaust Memories. Annihilation and Survival in Slovakia, by
Paul Davidovits

From Auschwitz with Love. The Inspiring Memoir of Two Sisters'
Survival, Devotion and Triumph Told by Manci Grunberger Beran &
Ruth Grunberger Mermelstein, by Daniel Seymour

Remetz. Resistance Fighter and Survivor of the Warsaw Ghetto, by Jan
Yohay Remetz

My March Through Hell. A Young Girl's Terrifying Journey to Survival,
by Halina Kleiner with Edwin Stepp

Roman's Journey, by Roman Halter

Beyond Borders. Escaping the Holocaust and Fighting the Nazis. 1938-
1948, by Rudi Haymann

The Engineers. A memoir of survival through World War II in Poland
and Hungary, by Henry Reiss

Memoirs by Elmar Rivosh, Sculptor (1906-1967). Riga Ghetto and
Beyond, by Elmar Rivosh

The series **Holocaust Survivor True Stories** consists of
the following biographies:

Among the Reeds. The true story of how a family survived the Holocaust,
by Tammy Bottner

A Holocaust Memoir of Love & Resilience. Mama's Survival from
Lithuania to America, by Ettie Zilber

Living among the Dead. My Grandmother's Holocaust Survival Story of
Love and Strength, by Adena Bernstein Astrowsky

Heart Songs. A Holocaust Memoir, by Barbara Gilford

Shoes of the Shoah. The Tomorrow of Yesterday, by Dorothy Pierce

Hidden in Berlin. A Holocaust Memoir, by Evelyn Joseph Grossman

Separated Together. The Incredible True WWII Story of Soulmates
Stranded an Ocean Apart, by Kenneth P. Price, Ph.D.

The Man Across the River. The incredible story of one man's will to
survive the Holocaust, by Zvi Wiesenfeld

If Anyone Calls, Tell Them I Died. A Memoir, by
Emanuel (Manu) Rosen

The House on Thrömerstrasse. A Story of Rebirth and Renewal in the
Wake of the Holocaust, by Ron Vincent

Dancing with my Father. His hidden past. Her quest for truth. How Nazi
Vienna shaped a family's identity, by Jo Sorochinsky

The Story Keeper. Weaving the Threads of Time and Memory - A
Memoir, by Fred Feldman

Krisia's Silence. The Girl who was not on Schindler's List, by
Ronny Hein

Defying Death on the Danube. A Holocaust Survival Story, by Debbie J.
Callahan with Henry Stern

A Doorway to Heroism. A decorated German-Jewish Soldier who
became an American Hero, by Rabbi W. Jack Romberg

The Shoemaker's Son. The Life of a Holocaust Resister, by
Laura Beth Bakst

The Redhead of Auschwitz. A True Story, by Nechama Birnbaum

Land of Many Bridges. My Father's Story, by Bela Ruth
Samuel Tenenholtz

Creating Beauty from the Abyss. The Amazing Story of Sam Herciger,
Auschwitz Survivor and Artist, by Lesley Ann Richardson

On Sunny Days We Sang. A Holocaust Story of Survival and Resilience,
by Jeannette Grunhaus de Gelman

Painful Joy. A Holocaust Family Memoir, by Max J. Friedman

I Give You My Heart. A True Story of Courage and Survival, by
Wendy Holden

In the Time of Madmen, by Mark A. Prelas

Monsters and Miracles. Horror, Heroes and the Holocaust, by
Ira Wesley Kitmacher

Flower of Vlora. Growing up Jewish in Communist Albania, by
Anna Kohen

Aftermath: Coming of Age on Three Continents. A Memoir, by Annette Libeskind Berkovits

Not a real Enemy. The True Story of a Hungarian Jewish Man's Fight for Freedom, by Robert Wolf

Zaidy's War. Four Armies, Three Continents, Two Brothers. One Man's Impossible Story of Endurance, by Martin Bodek

The Glassmaker's Son. Looking for the World my Father left behind in Nazi Germany, by Peter Kupfer

The Apprentice of Buchenwald. The True Story of the Teenage Boy Who Sabotaged Hitler's War Machine, by Oren Schneider

Good for a Single Journey, by Helen Joyce

Burying the Ghosts. She escaped Nazi Germany only to have her life torn apart by the woman she saved from the camps: her mother, by Sonia Case

American Wolf. From Nazi Refugee to American Spy. A True Story, by Audrey Birnbaum

Bipolar Refugee. A Saga of Survival and Resilience, by Peter Wiesner

Before the Beginning and After the End, by Hymie Anisman

Malka Owsiany recounts, by Mark Turkow (editor)

I Will Give Them an Everlasting Name. Jacksonville's Stories of the Holocaust, by Samuel P. Cox

The series **Jewish Children in the Holocaust** consists of the
following autobiographies of Jewish children
hidden during WWII in the Netherlands:

Searching for Home. The Impact of WWII on a Hidden Child, by
Joseph Gosler

See You Tonight and Promise to be a Good Boy! War memories, by
Salo Muller

Sounds from Silence. Reflections of a Child Holocaust Survivor,
Psychiatrist and Teacher, by Robert Krell

Sabine's Odyssey. A Hidden Child and her Dutch Rescuers, by
Agnes Schipper

The Journey of a Hidden Child, by Harry Pila and Robin Black

The series **New Jewish Fiction** consists of the following novels, written by Jewish authors. All novels are set in the time during or after the Holocaust.

The Corset Maker. A Novel, by Annette Libeskind Berkovits

Escaping the Whale. The Holocaust is over. But is it ever over for the next generation? by Ruth Rotkowitz

When the Music Stopped. Willy Rosen's Holocaust, by Casey Hayes

Hands of Gold. One Man's Quest to Find the Silver Lining in Misfortune, by Roni Robbins

The Girl Who Counted Numbers. A Novel, by Roslyn Bernstein

There was a garden in Nuremberg. A Novel, by Navina Michal Clemerson

The Butterfly and the Axe, by Omer Bartov

To Live Another Day. A Novel, Elizabeth Rosenberg

A Worthy Life. Based on a True Story, by Dahlia Moore

The series **Holocaust Heritage**
consists of the following memoirs by 2G:

The Cello Still Sings. A Generational Story of the Holocaust and of the
Transformative Power of Music, by Janet Horvath

The Fire and the Bonfire. A Journey into Memory, by Ardyn Halter

The Silk Factory: Finding Threads of My Family's True Holocaust Story,
by Michael Hickins

Hidden in Plain Sight. A Journey into Memory and Place, by Julie Brill

Against All Odds. A Memoir, by Grace Feuerverger

The series **Holocaust Books for Young Adults** consists of the
following novels, based on true stories:

The Boy behind the Door. How Salomon Kool Escaped the Nazis.
Inspired by a True Story, by David Tabatsky

Running for Shelter. A True Story, by Suzette Sheft

The Precious Few. An Inspirational Saga of Courage based on True
Stories, by David Twain with Art Twain

The series **WWII Historical Fiction** consists of the following novels, some of which are based on true stories:

Mendelevski's Box. A Heartwarming and Heartbreaking Jewish Survivor's Story, by Roger Swindells

A Quiet Genocide. The Untold Holocaust of Disabled Children in WWII Germany, by Glenn Bryant

The Knife-Edge Path, by Patrick T. Leahy

Brave Face. The Inspiring WWII Memoir of a Dutch/German Child, by I. Caroline Crocker and Meta A. Evenbly

When We Had Wings. The Gripping Story of an Orphan in Janusz Korczak's Orphanage. A Historical Novel, by Tami Shem-Tov

Jacob's Courage. Romance and Survival amidst the Horrors of War, by Charles S. Weinblatt

Join the AP Review Team

Reviews are very important in a world dominated by the social media. Feedback for Holocaust books is more than just a customer review; it also shows the relevance and importance of such books in today's society.

Please go over to the AmsterdamPublishers.com website (top of page) if you want to join the *AP review team*, showing **at least one review on Amazon** for one of our books. You will get updates about new releases and will get the chance to read and review.